I0559598

# Crossmaglen
# Paddy Said

## Patrick Joseph McEntegart

Copyright ©2023 by Patrick Joseph McEntegart.

ISBN 978-1-961254-68-8 (softcover)
ISBN 978-1-961254-69-5 (ebook)

All rights reserved. No part of this book may be reproduced or transmitted in any form or by any means, electronic or mechanical, including photocopying, recording, or by any information storage and retrieval system without express written permission from the author, except in the case of brief quotations embodied in critical reviews and certain other non-commercial uses permitted by copyright law.

This book is a work of fiction. Names, characters, places, and incidents are the product of the author's imagination or are used fictitiously. Any resemblance to actual locales, events, or persons, living or dead, is purely coincidental.

Printed in the United States of America.

INK START MEDIA
265 Eastchester Dr Ste 133 #102
High Point NC 27262

# Crossmaglen Paddy Said

Patrick Joseph McEntegart

# Crossmaglen Revelations

crossmaglen paddy saidis a factual account of an interview of a local man paddy an illiterate bachelor which began back in 1971 in crossmaglen when paddy was visited by an irish american writer. The writer paudric moore spent three days with paddy in intense study of the historic aspects of crossmaglen and beyond and upon leaving continued over the years since to maintain constant contact with paddy to help him pursue his dream for the betterment of crossmaglen. The second phase of moores novel transpires into a motivational inspiring story describing the pitfalls of the lives of both paddy and the writer. In the years since the 70's up to the present day and clearly demonstrate the dont quit phyosophy employed by both parties concerned

# In Memory of My Son Adrian

*Today, August 27th 1971, I Paudriac Moore stand at the threshold of the unknown. Before me lies a new venture and I'm going forward to take possession of it. I'm setting out on a journey to meet Paddy in a staunchly Irish Republican town on the Northern Irish border. Who knows what I will find? What new experiences or changes will come my way? What new needs will arise? In spite of all the uncertainty before me, I have a cheerful and comforting message from my dad: Paddy will take care of you.*

*I am departing from Woodlawn, New York, where I have lived all of my youthful 25 years in an Irish neighbourhood where I aspire to become a writer. My dad has organized this trip to help me brush up on my writing skills, and my mission is to interview a local man, Paddy, who is a Republican at heart. The town I am journeying to is presently fortified by a British Army garrison. My instructions are upon arrival to go directly to the Barrack Corner at the west end of the town square where Paddy awaits my arrival, sitting on his window sill and surveying events around him. After our meeting I am to pitch my tent in Urcher townland, east of the town, for my three-day stay in Crossmaglen.*

# Dedication

I dedicate all my efforts to date to my late mother "Katie", a truly wonderful woman who inspired me always from my tender years to become somebody. I am honoured to call her my best friend. We first met on a cold January day in 1946 and she has been my continued support ever since in my efforts to write. We have shared many of our life's experiences in the times we have known each other. She was the soul-mate , and was insistent that I continued to write. We are poor, she said, but stick to your schooling – I want you to make something of yourself when you grow up.

*On earth she toiled*

*Now in Heaven she rests*

*God bless you, "Katie"*

*You were one of the best*

# Acknowledgements

Brenda for her typing

Doug for brilliant craftsmanship

Melissa for her superb printing work

Siobhan for her professional attention to detail

Winifred for her photography and computer skills

# Disclaimer

*This book is for informational purposes only and is not intended for use as a source of legal, business, financial or professional advice. Readers are cautioned to rely on their own judgement about their individual circumstances and act accordingly. The author, printer, publisher shall have neither liability nor responsibility to any person or entity with respect to any loss or damage caused or alleged to be caused directly or indirectly by this book.*

Crossmaglen Paddy

# PREFACE

This book has a two-fold purpose: it sets out firstly to instil in its readers the importance of presenting our distinct cultural dialect in Crossmaglen and South Armagh the way it is. It is intended to rejuvenate the rural aspects of our culture by setting in place cottages for storytelling, poetry reading and traditional music and song combined with the preservation of our distinct local dialect.

For example, we don't say "speak", we say "spake", a word that can be found throughout the Bible – so we are not that far wrong. We don't say "door", we say "dure"; we don't say "cold", we say "cowl". Instead of saying "son" we might say "avik"; when addressing a boy, we would say "gasson" and a girl would be addressed as "gersha". We don't say "O'Neill", we say "O'Nale", and instead of "Shields", we say "Shales", which is the original spelling of these two names. This has been happening since the time of the Celts.

The second aim of this book is to generate the necessary funding to create a charitable centre in Crossmaglen for the benefit of the underprivileged in our community. It is also planned to initiate projects to benefit this disadvantaged area of Northern Ireland. .

If you wish to donate to this worthy cause please make checks payable to "Dunreavy" c/o Pat McEntegart 37 Lisseraw road Crossmaglen Newry Co Down N. Ireland BT359HT. thank you.,

This book is intended to trigger a positive spark in the lives and mind of all persons interested in equality and justice for all. The ordinary history of our country has been written by many, and the reader has a wide choice of narratives. But this book of mine has, for the first and only time, brought within reach of the general public a knowledge of the whole social life of Crossmaglen. In the simple, plain language of our community, it gives an account of the condition of our community in days now gone up to the present.

This is not a book to be read just for laughs as it contains a mix of tragedy and comedy, but it does fully capture the celebration of the Irish wit and language as practised in Crossmaglen. It is a true story and all events really happened as told. Upon meeting the older Paddy of Crossmaglen in 1971 and on hearing his stories, I wanted to write about the things he spoke of. It has taken me over 40 years to present them to the world but at last here it is, in honour of Crossmaglen and what Paddy had to say. Many of the dreams and visions we spoke of for Crossmaglen have come to full realisation in 2018. This book is one of them. I hope it brings you as much joy as it has brought me in writing it.

For example, we don't say "speak", we say "spake", a word that can be found throughout the Bible – so we are not that far wrong. We don't say "door", we say "dure"; we don't say "cold", we say "cowl". Instead of saying "son" we might say "avik"; when addressing a boy, we would say "gasson" and a girl would be addressed as "gersha". We don't say "O'Neill", we say "O'Nale", and instead of "Shields", we say "Shales", which is the original spelling of these two names. This has been happening since the time of the Celts.

*Crossmaglen Paddy Said* is a new collection of work, very revealing of my own inner thoughts. Through the years I have stopped and put down in writing some of the thoughts, feelings and emotions I have felt. My first serious attempt at writing for my own enjoyment, the book reflects my love of my native town Crossmaglen and its surrounding community and is also a collection of short writings entitled "stories". It is a lighter and more humorous insight into my experiences with friends in Crossmaglen that also gives voice to my native friends by writing about their lives from their perspective. Friends and relatives have suggested many times that I should write a book about my life, as it has been filled with what seems like more than a lifetime of experiences, although the final chapters have yet to unfold and be known. One day I might find the courage to relive these experiences and put them down for others to read, but for now I'm content to take a thought, a moment in time and write what I felt about it.

*Crossmaglen Paddy Said*, together with the songs, stories and poetry contained in it, are all works in progress, the progress being seen as a new thought comes forth from my mind and I find words to express it. Look for new additions in the future to all aspects of this book "Together in Development, Never Advocating Bigotry" (TIDNAB).

At this point I should explain some aspects of Irish Mythology.

Among all the Gallic peoples, generally speaking, there are three sets of men who are held in exceptional honour: the Bards, the Ovates and the Druids. The Bards are singers and poets, the Ovates are diviners and natural philosophers, while the Druids, in addition to natural philosophy, study also moral philosophy. (Strabo-Geographica first century AD)

In ancient times, many different chieftains, kings and queens ruled the lands we think of as Celtic today. But almost as powerful as those rulers were the Druids. These Druids were male and female, and in the Order they use the single term Druid as it has traditionally been used, to denote a person of either gender.

The mythology of pre-Christian Ireland did not entirely survive the conversion to Christianity. However, much of it was preserved in medieval Irish Literature, though it was shorn of its religious meanings. This literature represents the most extensive and best preserved of all the branches of Celtic Mythology.

Although many of the manuscripts have not survived and much more material was probably never committed to writing, there is enough

remaining to enable the identification of distinct, if overlapping cycles: The Mythological Cycle, the Ulster Cycle, the Fenian Cycle and the Historical Cycle. There is also a number of extant mythological texts that do not fit into any of the cycles. Additionally, there is a large number of recorded folk tales that, while not strictly mythological, feature personages from one or more of these four cycles.

In the Mythological Cycle, the Book of Invasions is a pseudo-history of Ireland which traces the ancestry of the Irish back to before the time of Noah. It tells of the invasion of Ireland by (among others) the people known as the Tuatha De Dannan. With the arrival of the Gaels, the Tuatha De Dannan retired underground to become the fairy people of later myth and legend. Some of their folklore still exists in South Armagh at this present time. (Irish Mythology Wikipedia)

# GLOSSARY OF TERMS

| Instead of | Some might say |
|---|---|
| Cold | Cowl |
| Shields | Shales |
| O'Neill | O'Nale |
| Path | Pad |
| Speak | Spake |
| Boy | Gasson |
| Girl | Gersa |
| Door | Dure |
| A bad day | Bruckely weather |
| Lane | Lonin |
| Floor | Flure |
| Kettle | Kittle |
| Drain | Shuck |
| Sure | Shure |
| Decent | Dacent |
| Potatoes | Praties/spuds |
| Told | Towel |
| Upon my soul | Pon me sowel |
| A good person | A dacent crater |
| Looking | Luckin |
| Children | Childer |
| Mean | Mane |
| Peace | Pace |
| Deal | Dale |
| Child | Chile |
| **Son** | **avick** |
| **Lane** | **lonin** |

# The Crossmaglen Community in Bygone Days

The community Paddy lived in was one of deep Christian faith. When I was growing up, it didn't matter who came into our house during the family rosary; we weren't ashamed to be seen on our knees. The visitor would join us just like family. Grace was said before meals and after meals in every home before and after meals. When you were leaving the house, you would apply holy water to your forehead, and in the fields even the horses in the plough would stand for the angelus bell. No servile work was done on Sundays except in the case of severe weather when permission was granted from the altar. There was no stealing or damaging of property, and murder was something that happened in another country. The mode of transport in my young days was mostly bicycles or pony and trap, and in Crossmaglen during markets or football matches and masses, there would be thousands of bicycles on the Square. There was no need for locks. When cars became common, you would never pass any neighbour walking on the road. When I got my first Morris Minor van, I never took the keys out of the ignition in the local area for the ten years I had it. Homes were never locked at night and people supported any neighbour in need. They maintained roads, built churches, schools, playing fields and clubs, produced their own food and educated famous children.

All those things are still being practised – nobody has the right to kill off a culture. How in God's name could this be a bad place based on a background like that?

The only work the police had to do in this community was to enforce environmental issues such as cutting the ragworts and licensing of dogs—there was no crime. From what I learned it was quite different from NY---so--I did arise and I went there and I prayed that Cross I'd see."I Paudric Moore grew up in the Irish neighbourhood of Woodlawn, New York, where our sports were Gaelic football in Paddy's field and Gaelic Park in the Bronx each evening and weekend, together with trips to the Irish festivals in Queens and Manhattan. Each summer we spent in the Catskills mountains in our cottage where more festivals took place. I studied at Lehman College in the Bronx and went swimming in Valhalla Dam upstate. Our family was traditional Irish. My life revolved around my studies to become a mechanical engineer and I spent much of my time in my room aspiring to become a writer. My dad encouraged me to pursue this interest and suggested a trip to Ireland to brush up my skills. This was in the late 1960's and he was concerned about the level of unrest in Northern Ireland and in particular in Crossmaglen, his birthplace, so =therefore he was organizing a trip for me to go there. So there I was, me, Paudraic Moore all packed up and ready to leave New York via Kennedy Airport en route to Dublin Airport. I had my notes for my assignment in Ireland which had been handed to me by my father who was sending me to Crossmaglen, South Armagh, to meet up with a local man, Paddy. My instructions were to create a set of circumstances for finding permanent work for myself in Crossmaglen – "But make sure you don't ask questions directly," Dad said. "Talk in riddle formation!"

"Talk with Paddy; he'll keep you right," Dad said.

When I arrived at Dublin Airport, I took a bus to Connolly Train Station where I boarded the northbound train for Dundalk, County Louth, where I fetched a train schedule which outlined my route. The schedule outlined some stops relevant to Crossmaglen but I was unsure as to which one to get off at. I had a question for the conductor who answered nervously; in fact, he also appeared to get increasingly pale around his cheekbones because of my question.

Our train was the 7.40 express from Dublin to Belfast in Northern Ireland. I noticed its reduction in speed as we crossed the Boyne River bridge at Drogheda, County Louth. Availing of the reduction in noise levels while I surveyed the upcoming stops on my colourful schedule, I beckoned the conductor's attention. It was Saturday evening in late August, very late, August 29th, and the year was 1971. I said, "Sir, I'm slightly confused," and recognising that I was an American tourist he came quickly to my assistance with a jovial welcome and enquired as to the nature of my problem.

"Well, not a problem, exactly," I said. "It's more in the nature of a challenge. You see, my father has told me I have a brilliant future ahead of me and he has wagered a substantial bet with his colleagues in America that I will find an abundance of work in the town of Crossmaglen in South Armagh. Do you think I should disembark your train at Dundalk or Newry, Mr Conductor?"

The island of Ireland is positioned in the Atlantic Ocean in such a way as to warrant its continuous share of strong, penetrating winds which have the general tendency to beat on the outer extremes of the human body, thereby causing a reddish facial colouring in some of its citizens exposed to it. I watched dumbfounded as the three-inch diameter cheek areas on my conductor friend's face began to rapidly change to a pale white. Was it something I should have tipped him for in advance, or was it religious? Perhaps he had a heart condition; he looked shocked!

Eventually he regained his composure. "Are you having me on, Yank?" he asked, somewhat hesitantly. "Is it codding me you are?" he repeated.

"No, sir," I said, "this is my mission here tonight, to travel to Crossmaglen, looking for work."

He retired to the dining car some distance away and returned minutes later with a glass or rather a half glass of water in his hand. Some of the colour had returned to his cheeks so I presumed he had most likely drank the missing contents. An exact half glass of water is what he set on the train table in front of me.

"Now I have a question for you, my visiting friend from America," he said to me with some confidence returning to his voice.

"Okay, sir," I said, "that's fair. What is your question?"

"Is the glass half empty or is it half full?"

I analysed what was in front of me. I wondered if it had been measured exactly, and if so, how many attempts it took to extract the first half of its contents to leave a vibrant, half-full glass remaining.

"It's half full, Mr Conductor," I said.

"Okay, my friend. We'll be in Dundalk in four minutes. Get a taxi to Crossmaglen; it's about 7 or 8 miles. But remember this: if you ask the boyo's around Crossmaglen if the glass is half full or half empty, they'll probably tell you the glass is the wrong bloody size. Good luck."

Not long after I was almost there, me, Paudriac Moore, on my way to Crossmaglen, South Armagh, in a taxi cab from Dundalk train station. We travelled along the Castleblaney road for four miles. The driver spoke little, and the road was dark, preventing me from viewing the countryside. A short distance past Annavacky for Crossmaglen, the driver made a right turn. He said we would soon reach the border. The road was bumpy and narrow. My driver explained that there was not even a border crossing sign; the only visible sign was one of an uneven road surface with some huge concrete bollards strewn along the sides of the road by a small stream which divided the townlands of Drumakavall and Courtbane.

After crossing the stream we continued north for a mile and a half. It was dark so I couldn't see the layout of the landscape. Very soon I saw a 30-mile per hour speed limit sign on the side of a hill approaching with a sign in Gaelic welcoming me to Crossmaglen. Then we passed St Joseph's High School on our left.and next came Crossmaglen Rangers Gaelic Football Grounds as we approached the public square. Then midway along the eastern top side of the Square at the junction of the Culloville road was what's famously known as the "Barrack Corner". There the taxi came to a halt, right alongside a British Army observation lookout post. I noticed that the street lighting wasn't working and everywhere was in darkness except for the lights coming from the buildings. As I exited the cab and retrieved my rucksack from the boot I noticed a man seated on the corner window sill he wore a tweed cap and gray gaberdeen overcoat. I correctly assumed it was Paddy so I stuck out my hand to greet him as I stepped across the uneven paving stones in the footpath, I noticed how uneven the street pavements were. They appeared to have been ripped up by force. Paddy explained that they had been used in anger as missiles to throw at the nearby army barracks on the night of August the 15th , the day after the shooting dead of the local father of three, Harry Thornton. As I closed the taxi door I could make out hordes of people assembling on the footpath close to the Barrack Corner in an angry mood, close by on the town square an Ulsterbus was being set alight by more youths, next to the barrack gates on the Cullaville road crowds were filing around in ringed formation praying the rosary, on the barrack lawn the police sergants car was

4

upended and set alight and stone throwers began smashing up the barrack front the mood was one of anger at the forces of law and order Paddy said they were reacting to the burning out of their homes of some 1500 catholics the previous week in Bombay street Belfast, some of the refugees made it as far as Newtownhamilton & Crossmaglen and at the same time civil rights activists John Hume/Austin Currie/and Ivon Cooper held a public meeting in the local hall to launch a rent&rates strike. Paddy relayed all this to me as the roits continued outside the barracks.

Paddy spoke in a broad Irish dialect which instantly reminded me of a paragraph from Part One of Canto I of "The Hudibras", a poem written by Samuel Butler in 1859. edited by Henry George Bohn For my money, that best describes Paddy's speech:

> *but, when he pleas'd to shew't, his speech was*
> *"In loftiness of sound was rich;*
> *A Babylonish dialect;*
> *Which learned pedants much affect"*
> *It was a party coloured dress of patch'd and py-ball'd languages.:*
> *Twas {Irish} cut on Greek and Latin, like fustian heretofore on satin.*
> *It had an odd promiscuous tone, as if he had talked three parts in one;*
> *Which made some think, when he did gabble,*
> *Th, had heard three laborers of Babel;*
> *Or Cerberus himself announce*
> *A leash of languages at once.*

I knew I was in for a rare treat – but exactly how rare, I could not have guessed. Come to Crossmaglen, dear reader, come to the Barrack Corner, Crossmaglen, pull up a stool and meet the people. Your life will never be the same again.

I should at this point explain that the early stages of this story are centred on my arrival in Crossmaglen late in the evening of August 29th, 1971, and it is based on the events of the next three days as we moved around the town from place to place. Sometimes we were in Shorts pub in North Street, and other times we were in St. Patrick's Church in Newry Street or in "The Glen Cafe" on the Square. The remainder of the story concerns the experiences of Paddy and myself up to the present day.

Paddy began filling his Peterson pipe while I removed my rucksack from my back.

"Did you ate lately, avick?"

"No, Paddy, I had a coffee on the train, that's all."

"Well, get yourself down across that square to Gerry's Glen Cafe and tell Gerry I sent you. Gerry will take it from there. I have another wee errand to do; only for that I'd be with you. Make yourself at home in the Glen Cafe with Gerry, yer in safe hands with him. I'll be back to meet you before you're finished eating. Put your rucksack into the back of my ould van there and it'll be safe enough."

I headed off across the Square towards the Glen Café. It was raining. Gerry greeted me with a hearty hello as I entered the café. I told him who I was and that I was with Paddy.

"Grab yourself a chair there, gasson, and we'll have ye fed in no time. You're welcome to Cross."

As I got myself a table by the window I noticed that there was a green coloured bus pulling up outside the café. It had a gold stripe along its side and County Clare number plates on it. Very soon the occupants of the bus were pouring out on the footpath by the café, which they proceeded to enter post haste.

"Come on in," Gerry said, "we were expecting yous. Had yous a safe trip?"

"Well, the diesel pump went on us in Kildare, but we got going again." There were about 40 of them in all, and pretty soon the café was crowded. There was even more activity outside on the square, with cars and vans dropping off picks and shovels and yard brushes. More men came into the café from the cars and one man introduced himself as Peter John Carraher. The spokesman for the visitors was Martin Calligan, who together with his close friend Jimmy Keane had organized the busload to come to Crossmaglen to help fill in the border crossings which the Brits had created by using explosives to open huge craters on all cross-border roads in South Armagh. This had been done on purpose to inconvenience local people north and south of the border, some of whom had farm land and livestock on both sides of it. This deliberate act of inconveniencing the farmers and business persons on both sides forced the natives to travel many extra miles in a detour to get to their destination. These border crossings, before they were blown up, had been important links to cross-border trade by businesses going backward and forward with goods and services and farm animals all the time. "Yis are all very welcome, men," Peter John said. "We'll start at Drumlougher. It's the worst." Just then the phone rang. Gerry answered it, and when he hung up he turned to the group and said, "That was The Roadstone Quarry in Castleblaney They are going to keep their quarry open all night to help with the road filling."

Next to pull in was a grey Morris Minor van 762 EOL. It was Paddy returning from his errand. Very soon everyone was fed and all meals were on the house, courtesy of Gerry. Then the picks and shovels were loaded onto the Clare

7

bus and the convoy headed for the border. I travelled with Paddy in his van and when we arrived at the first site, the area around the crater was floodlit with spotlights. Work went on during the night and God bless the women of South Armagh who kept the soup and sandwiches supplied all night. By daylight the goal had been reached: All the border crossings were again open to passing traffic. Paddy left me at my appointed campsite in Wrights Lane and I said I'd see him after I got some sleep, I had just experienced first-hand the "people's rule in South Armagh".

After some few hours' sleep, I fetched some water from a nearby spring well, washed and had some coffee, then headed off walking on the one-mile journey into Crossmaglen. I went along up Caffney's Brea in through the hamlet of Monog, through the area known locally as the Dirty Hollow and climbed steadily from the east into Crossmaglen Square at the lower end. I was pleasantly surprised on my way into town by the very scenic views I had all around me. The contours of the landscape were ever changing and the fabulous views of the Slieve Gullion mountains were a sight to behold. Even the cattle grazing in the fields came alongside the roadway to greet me and the people out on their morning stroll stopped for a friendly quick hello.

It's no wonder Crossmaglen and South Armagh in general is designated as an area of "outstanding beauty".

The first I saw as I approached the Square was the cattle mart building in the centre, with its steel-railed pens attached to its north side.

Then to my right along the north end of the Square I saw Crossmaglen Courthouse, an impressive triple-arched two storey stone building with an east-facing clock and belfry.

I veered west at an angle towards the Barrack Corner by the junction of the Culloville road where Paddy was clearly positioned beneath this solid, two-storey structure. Formerly known as "Lennon's Alehouse", it was an inn for weary travellers along the post road from Dundalk to Castleblaney in the 1600's.It is now a dwelling house with a chemist shop on the ground floor next to the Barrack Corner. James Lennon came to that spot in 1600 and established an Inn at the crossroads which became known as "The Cross of Lennon", which in the Gaelic tongue was "Cros-O-Ma-Gleannan", later anglicised to Crossmaglen in the 18th century..

This was day two of my visit to "Cross", as Paddy called it. It was Friday and that meant it was the Fair day so there would be a lot of activity all day.

I crossed the roadway on my approach to Paddy's stand (or seat) and cheerfully bade him good morning, to which he returned my compliment.

Just then I heard the sound of an army saraceen car being driven out of the army base . I looked westward out the Cullaville road whetre a convoy of soldiers were lining up each side of the road. The saraceen moved onto the roadway facing the town square followed by the C.O of the regiment. The patrol marched menacingly towards the Barrack Corner and the square with the C.O. out in front as if inviting confrontation with the locals who were passing by. When he arrived at the corner he immediately went to Paddy and asked him "who was doing all the shooting around these parts mate"? I'm not your mate! Paddy snapped back at him! I/m just punching time here every day minding me own business----hear nothing---see nothing—know nothing-----that's what you all say in this town----it's all hush hush but this town is full of republican sympathizers but I'll change all that before I leave here the C.O. said----a lighter job would suit ye "avick" Paddy said----bigger min than ye tried that on and where did it get them?----with that the C.O. backed off and began to retreat towards the army base.

"I'll just tell yeh right away, gasson," Paddy said, "the way it is right now with us in Cross, we are hard-pressed on every side, but not crushed; perplexed, but not in despair; persecuted, but not abandoned; struck down, but never destroyed.

"As human beings most of us have a strong desire to be free, free to make our own decisions and opinions, to choose our friends, partners and careers and to essentially drive the course of our own lives. But the sad truth is around these parts, avick, for the majority of this population, total freedom is a far-off dream. Have yeh ever felt like this? Do you often find yourself wishing you could break past the restrictions in your life, to finally achieve total time freedom like we wish for here in Crossmaglen!"

Just then there was a very loud "thud", much louder than the one I made banging the rear door of the taxi cab the previous evening. Luckily for the scared driver I had paid him his fare of four pounds and ten shillings before we entered the large market square. Then came another "thud", much louder, followed by a parish chorus of the canine vocals. Smoke began rising from behind some buildings. There were no humans outdoors, except one couple, and I was one half of that couple. Standing at the Barrack Corner was a lone figure (Paddy) with a bare head, Paddy had his cap in his hand, he was praying out loud: "Lord, give me wisdom to direct me ways, I beg no riches nor yet length of days. Me life is a flower the time it has to last, is mixed with 'frost' and shuck with every blast."

What we were witnessing was a mortar attack on the British Army barracks by the Provisional Irish Army. After the dust and smoke had settled, the British began moving slowly from their fortress towards the Square in Saracen armoured cars. There were also some foot soldiers on both sides of the Culloville road. They moved nervously, ignoring our presence at the Barrack Corner

"Give it to me straight, Paddy," I said, being the bloody eejit I was, asking a Crossmaglen man a question and expecting a straight answer no less. "What's at stake here, Paddy?"

"Well, I'll jus tell ye, avick. It's like this. Do ye see where that tobacco spit of mine jus landed, gasson?"

I nodded in silence. Well, give me a little credit for a small piece of intelligence! Sure, I nodded in silence; this was no time to interrupt him.

"That spot where me spit landed, that's the ancient pivotal centre of the Celtic centre which encompasses Crossmaglen, South Armagh, in the Baroney of the Fews in Ireland, avick, and as long as we are in the centre of this circle, gasson, there's divil the stranger" – by which he meant the British soldiers – "is going to convince us that we're only a small cog in the wheel of events that occur round these parts, gasson. How could they maintain they were in control of things, when we created the whole circle of events?"

I reached for my bottle of pure spring water. No, I hadn't developed a thirst, I just needed some help swallowing my first lesson in Crossolegy, as Paddy termed it.

"Pon me sowel, avick, ye took that on your chin rightly. Do ye know what I'm going to tell ye, gasson? Yer standing there gazing into the window of opportunity. Pon me sowel, avick, yer howlin the kays to free yourself. Is it work I heard ye saying ye were lucking for? Trow yourself into yer work with enthusiasm and am telling ye, you'll prove that we are not the small cog around these parts, an you'll make a few dollars for yerself into the bargain, an fair play to ye, gasson. De blessins of God be with ye and all yer childer."

It was then I began to realize the abundance of work I had stumbled upon in Crossmaglen. My work would be to write Paddy's story and eventually turn it into a book – that was it, that's what my father had seen when he placed his wager of $1000 on me finding work when I came to Crossmaglen! Bingo! I had hit the jackpot.

Paddy said he had it "on authority from his great-grandfather Pauderdean that Oliver Wendell Holmes was sitting at the hearthstone in Lennon's Ale House in Crossmaglen a few centuries back, waiting for his overcoat to dry by the fireside, when he penned the following description of what he heard going on around him:

> *When I think of my Country –*
> *I express what I am,*
> *anchoring my roots.*
> *and this is what the heart tells,*
> *as if a hidden frontier ran from me to others,*
> *embracing us all within a past*
> *older than each of us;*
> *and from this past I emerge*
> *when I think my country,*
> *I take her into me as a treasure,*
> *constantly wondering how to increase it,*
> *how to give a wider measure to that space*
> *it fills withal.*

Karol Wojtyla (Polish)

# Paddy - The engineer
# Specifications for a good engineer

"A good engineer must be flexible, sober, truthful, accurate, resolute, discreet and be of cool and sound judgement. He must have integrity and command of his temper; he must have the courage to resist and repel attempts at intimidation, and a firmness that is proof against solicitation, flattery or improper bias of any kind. He must take interest in his work. He must be energetic, quick to decide and prompt to act; he must be as fair and impartial as a judge on a bench, have experience in his work with men, which implies some maturity of years, and he must have business habits and knowledge of accounts."

# Functions of a surveyor

When conducting an original survey, it is the function of the surveyor to make a perfect survey, establish permanent monuments and true markings and make a correct record of his work in the form of field notes and a plat.

Okay, fair enough – except for a couple of important items. I am to record notes regarding a plot of land 365 feet above sea level, midway along the western side of the second largest Market Square in Europe, but there's a slight technicality: this particular "Square", in fact, according to my research notes, is not a square at all; it's a rectangle. My financiers for this expedition are a group of "Bardic Explorers" who claim that the rectangular system of subdividing lands, adopted by the US Congress on May 20th, 1785, was first employed by the "Celtic Druids" on the ancient site of my upcoming project.

According to my instructors, the first public land surveys to use the rectangle system were made in the eastern part of the present state of Ohio under the direction of Captain Thomas Hutchin.

I have been informed that acts of Congress approved on May 18th 1796, again on May 10th 1800, revised on February 11th 1805, and updated on through revised instructions issued in 1855, that it is obviously impossible to preserve a true rectangular system on a spherical, owing to the convergence of meridians. Let me clarify that one. By way of preparing you for this expedition, I'll use the letters A, L and M. The angular convergence A of two meridians is M sin L, where M is the mean latitude of two positions and sin or sine is the ratio of the side opposite a given angle in a right-angled triangle to the hypotenuse – are you still with me? Okay. Now if you accept Webster's definition of *meridian* as being "the highest point of power, prosperity, splendour" etc., and you convert the previously used letters A, L and M into the three Irish counties of Armagh, Louth and Monaghan, by locating their meeting point on your personal map of Ireland, you will find your pointer in the townland of Rassan right on the ancient landmark of "Ferdana" bush, along the Derry/Dublin road midway between the towns of Dundalk and Castleblaney. Because my notes will be a record of a resurvey, original landmarks such as "Federna" are vital to its accuracy. My eventual detailed focus, however, will be on a much disputed "Corner" three miles further north on your Irish map, i.e. the Barrack Corner, Crossmaglen Anxious to broaden my knowledge of "Corners", my Bardic instructors once more referred me to the act of Congress from which the following description is taken:

"Corners"

"the corner monument may be as follows:

(A) stone with pits and earthen mounds;
(B) stone with mound of stone;
(C) stone with bearing trees;
(D) post in mound of earth;
(E) post in mound of stone;
(F) post with bearing trees;
(G) simple mound of earth and stone;
(H) tree without bearing trees;
(I)  tree with bearing trees;
(J)  rock in place etc.

An obliterated corner is one where no visible evidence remains of the work of the original surveyor in establishing it. Its location may, however, have been preserved beyond all question by the acts of landowners, and by the memory of those who knew and recollect the true position of the original monument. In such cases it is not a lost corner. A lost corner is one whose position cannot be determined beyond reasonable doubt, either from original marks or reliable external evidence.

Paddy said that his schoolmaster friend towel him they had researched this information from various libraries from the land surveyor reference manual by Andrew L Harbin.

In war-torn Northern Ireland in the early 1970's, this might not prove all too easy. I was informed that the Chief' Surveyor's name was Paddy and Paddy required an assistant to take notes.

"You'll find him on his 'Stone'," my Dad told me, "and you are to pitch tent in a certain location known as Wright's Lane. This is required because of its unique position in relation to the rising sun. Paddy will explain and record everything in minute detail. Good luck."

My work assignment entailed pinpointing the exact location of "Lennon's Alehouse Crossmaglen Eurigena" (L.A.C.E.), which is the present location known as the Barrack Corner. James Lennon in the early 1600's constructed an Inn at a then crossroads in Crossmaglen, which became famous as the "cross of Lennon". In the Gaelic tongue it was Cros-oh-ma Gleannan.

Those were all the instructions I received.

# Paddy on Spelling & Grammar

"By the way, just in case any of ye are thinking of complaining about the spelling or the odd missing coma, or for that matter, if some of you happen to spot wee letters where you know there should be big long lanky ones, pass no remarks. James Joyce never worried about his spelling; Joyce maintained people always understood what he was trying to get across."

"There was a very learned gentleman by the name of Theodore Marton back in the Fifties who was trying to solve some of the problems of life in outer space. Marton lived in America somewhere out around Princeton University in New Jersey, and yer man Marton was at the same time trying to solve another problem in relation to what was the right way to spell words."

Paddy continued, "There were a whole crowd of experts gathering books and things from high schools and colleges all over the place and he knew some of their names, too. According to what I was towel, avick, there was a woman be the name of Mary Elting, and she employed an assistant by the name of Mrs Lore Phillips, and together they wrote a book that they spoke, but they did not write it or read it. Those who lived in the eastern part did not always pronounce their words in the same ways. This is true in America, too. Some people in the west say 'idea' and 'butter', but when people in Boston use the same words, they say 'idear' and 'buttah'. You can guess what happened when writing finally came to England. Each person spelled words the way they pronounced them. Spelling got still more mixed up after England was conquered by the Normans who had a different language and their own way of writing down sounds. All of this happened before the invention of printing. At that time books had to be copied by hand. Each person who copied a book spelled as they pleased. Nobody cared as long as the meaning was clear. "The first book printers began to use regular ways of spelling some words, and the people who wrote books thought this was a good idea. Still, if a printer wanted to make a line come out even so that the page would look neat, he might add or subtract a letter here or there. For example, he would use *knowe* or *kenowe* or *know*. The people who made dictionaries picked and chose the spellings they liked. At last, about two hundred years ago, almost all dictionary makers and teachers and printers began to agree on some rules.

There seems to be no reason why they kept some of the odd and unreasonable spellings. Perhaps they hated to change old habits. Perhaps they just liked the way the words looked.

"Long ago writers did not use any periods or commas or question marks or any other punctuation marks. Then printers began to divide up words. They used punctuation marks, and they were the ones who gave us pages that were easy to read. It didn't make a happer of difference to meself. I couldn't make a trick out of anything they wrote, and furthermore, gasson, just in case all the women of the world start heading for the Barrack Corner in Cross accusing me of being politically incorrect, let me tell them, avick, that these are not my words, they belong to a woman by the name of Mary Elting "P.S. Don't bother yer heads to write complaining to Paddy either—waste of your precious time, God bless yis, and may the road always rise up to meet yis."

The following pointers from Paddy may assist readers on their journey through these rambling South Armagh pages.If you happen to encounter difficulty with any of the big, long words ahead of you, it might be beneficial to keep in mind the technique employed by the newspaper readers of Crossmaglen, South Armagh, Ireland at the turn of the twentieth century. As Paddy explained, "They were the Dalin Men from Crossmaglen who travelled all over Ireland to horse and cattle fairs, and they were absent from home for long periods of time. Their return would always be an occasion for much excitement, and mass congregations were guaranteed to assemble in their various homes.

These gatherings were initiated by excited brethren, eager to hear the news from afar in matters of trade and commerce, and "scandal"

"James was one of these dalin men, and he arrived home at the top of Lissaraw Fort and informed his news-thirsty audience that he would be in Lennon's after milking time the next night to demonstrate his skills in extracting stories from within the pages of *The Irish Nation* newspaper. It was November, and the evenings were very dark. Country cottages had small windows; the hurricane lamp would be lit early, it sat on the table. James began reading. That was no problem since he was the only one who could make a stammer at it, and every time James came to a big, long word, he would call to the women of the house to 'Screw up the Lamp'. After this slight pause James would then begin at the other end of the big word, and nobody was any the wiser that James had skipped the difficult word."

So, readers, be warned: You may at times find yourself employing James' tactic as you ramble o'er these South Armagh pages.

Paddy stood up – no, it was not to worship me; my father had schooled me well before I left New York. "Watch out for the jesters," he warned me repeatedly, "take note of the shin scratching, and the nose pulling." I was taking such a note now.

Paddy was viewing my preoccupation while at the same time he massaged his right shinbone with the steel toe-cap of his left Shamrock brand leather boot. According to my external sources back home, this ritual I was witnessing would go under the heading of 'Crytocheironomy', or to make it easier on readers, 'Ogham Gestures'. Dad had said there were two forms I should look out for. Dad had a friend in New York who had done some research in ancient Celtic customs, and this friend had explained that Cos-ogam (leg ogam) is a method of communicating by gesticulating with the shin bone as the Ogam stem line. Dad and his friend told me the gesticulator would be forming letters with his fingers on both sides of his body. Luckily for me my Dad had placed a copy of R.A. Stewart Macalister's text of "The secret languages of Ireland" into my rucksack, saying it will come in handy for you in Crossmaglen. The text describes a prearranged code of manual gestures known as crytocheironomy. Members of secret societies make much use of this method of secret conversation. Just then a small pipe-smoking man approached the corner where Paddy was seated---not a bad day men---he said-----well Barney,, what's the craic Paddy said----how's yer father?---mugatin nid'es grani(s) mwilsa (the fool does not understand me) Barney said in a strange accent----I deduced that this was a form of the ancient Shelta language constructed by the Irish travellers where they turned the words backwards to conceal the message from the strangers----just then a shawl wearing female passed by heading south along the footpath. Stesh charp minkur btser, granhe her gredhurn (that's a true tinker woman, I know by her face) Paddy said again in this strange tongue. I was now taking note of the hand gestures of both men at the corner and I was recalling something I had read about ogam letters suitable for spelling out words and sentences by means of finger-signs. The number of the groups of scores, from one to five, suggest the hand and its fingers, all these letters, including the group of complex characters at the end of the row, can be made with one hand or both, held in various attitudes and with as many fingers outstretched as may be required. The text continues by stating that evidently this is a convenient device for secret communication, semi illiterate audience, could conceal their thoughts in perfect security, they could even secretly contradict what they were saying openly, by word of mouth. The alphabet was originally intended as a manual sign alphabet. When we examine it closely we see that its construction is very far from childish, there is learning behind it. Its inventor knows the difference between vowels and consonants---indeed it is the only European alphabet which resembles the wonderful monument of phonetic analysis, the Deranagari script, in keeping those groups of sound-symbols apart.

Barney then sat down beside Paddy---he had a stick with him and he retreaved a penknife from his waistcoat pocket and began nicking notches on his stick----that's a birch rod gasson he said,.the first thing ever written in ogam was seven strokes cut on a birch rod, which warned the mythical hero Lug mac Ethlenn that his wife would be carried off seven times to fairyland unless she were protected by birch. At that point an elderly lady approached the corner carrying two bags of groceries----well Paddy ----more power till yeh----muscha sheary----muscha sheary,she said repeatedly. I went to my notes then and found that muscha is Celtic for ah well---and sheary is Celtic for peace .While all this was going on I began studying the text on the secret languages and found in chapter 2 the subject of cryptology which was defined As the art whereby two persons, A and B, interchange a communication, while withholding its purport from a third person Z.This may take the form of speech (overheard by Z) which may be secret (a) because the language is unknown, or (b) because the words are used with unknown meanings; then in Cryptoglossy A and B speak in a language unknown to Z. The language used may be some actual but little known tongue; or artificial jargon, slang,or argot.Just then some youths passed by on their way to the football club to the south. I could make out that they were using some strange words in their discourse with each other----words like de feen/ de byor/sooblik/and lackin---I went to my notes where I found a heading on the Shelta language spoken by Irish travellers which explained that de feen was the man---de byor was a woman---sooblik was a boy/and lackin was a girl-----the youths used other words like munyah and rulyah---munyah being great and rulyah being crazy.It was obvious that this ancient secret language was still alive in Crossmaglen in the 70's.

Paddy scratched himself, shook himself, then adjusted the peak of what was once a very fashionable tweed cap, though the fastener of its peak had long been displaced. Then he applied the index finger of his left hand to his nose in vertical movements. He had previously been compacting tobacco in his clay pipe with the same finger, and the red goose pimples on Paddy's weather-beaten nose began to turn. Falling back on my mental research notes on the subject of 'Sron-ogam' (nose-ogam), I could recall Dad's friend having warned me that the ridge of the nose could be employed in the same way as the shin bone by the applicant of these ancient codes.

"So tell me, gasson," Paddy said, as he pared a birch stick with his penknife, with which he seemed to be cutting ringed grooves approximately one inch apart into the short, hand-held stick, "is it work yer looking for? Is that what I heard ye saying? You came all the way from America to try yer hand at sorting this whole mess out. Well, the blessins of God be with ye and may ye never see a poor day. Will ye be looking for help? Do ye think ye have enough lead in that pencil of ye?"

I could remember another title from my childhood which my Granda Pat Lennon used to relay about the antics of the boyos around Cross. "Codology" he called it.

"Not at all, avick, where did ye hear that? It's *Cross*ology, gasson!"

In the illustrious library in Trinity College, Dublin, bound in a cover with the mark H2 15, there is contained a document which was completed on the 5th of May 1643. It is in two parts. In the second part, there is a single sheet of paper in legible handwriting from the pen of an Irish historian of the time which contains a list of somewhat obscure words not commonly found or used in everyday communications between peoples of English-speaking countries.

Paddy was noting my puzzlement. There was a certain glint in his left eye.

"Hey, ye boy ye. Do ye think we'll have enough work for ye, avick, around Cross?" he said, as his clay pipe ping-ponged around his toothless jaws. "Pon me sowel, ye might have more courage than sense, gasson".

The aforementioned book has an Irish reference juxtaposed to each obscure word which are set into individual columns, two on each page. At the top of the first page there is a very descriptive title.

"*Duil Laithne and so sios* (a book of Latin here below). Pon me sowel, but ye were digging brave and deep to find out how we spake round here, avick."

I hadn't opened my mouth at this time but Dad had warned me, "There's boyos round Cross can read your mind."

This book, *Duil Laithne*, makes reference to a secret language recorded back in the ninth or tenth century by Cormac mac Cuillennain, and it appears to describe 'the speech called Ogham'.

Paddy fixed his gaze upon me once more. What was happening here? Nobody spoke. Well, I was determined not to ask questions; there was no point. "Be patient," Dad had said. Apparently this ancient language of signs, signals, riddles and diversions was still alive in Cross. I wondered what other and how many strange secrets this place held. Where would I begin? How would I begin? Where would it all end? Would it ever end? When would I know?

"Didn't ye say it was work ye were looking for, avick? De blessins of God be on ye, gasson."

"I hold every man a debtor to his profession, from the which as men of course do seek to receive countenance and profit, so ought they of duty to endeavour themselves, by way of amends, to be a help and ornament thereunto."

So said Francis Bacon, the English renaissance statesman and philosopher, best known for his promotion of the scientific method, at some point between 1561 and 1626. Well, that was then and this was now and Bacon was dead and I was standing at the Barrack Corner in Cross and for all I knew I could be joining Bacon very shortly. I swallowed hard. In fact, I felt it might be an infringement upon Paddy were I to spit out. Actually I was glad of the saliva in my mouth because it was still very dry. You're laughing, but this was 1971 in strongly Republican territory in Northern Ireland. I was a long ways from 41$^{st}$ and 5$^{th}$ Avenue in New York City, where the words of Wendell L Willkie, the US Republican presidential candidate who became famous with his «One World» concept of international cooperation, were erected by 'Freedom House' in February 1957:

"I believe in America," he wrote,

*Because in it we are free, free to choose our government to speak our minds to observe our different religions"*

It couldn't happen ever again, "not in a month of Sundays", as they say around Crossmaglen. I was surveying the Crossmaglen rendition of a star of David type logo, chiselled into the concrete sidewalk at the Barrack Corner, which had just been highlighted by brown lubricants from Paddy's tobacco saliva. I thought perhaps the mark might have some kind of engineering significance, the kind of benchmark surveyors are prone to leave as a future reference. I should have known better, or more to the point, I should have remembered my dad's advice to me on leaving New York. "They'll read what you're thinking in your mind," Dad had said.

"Yer puzzled, gasson," Paddy observed. "It has ye confused. Yer forehead is full of questions. I could plant small praties in the lines across yer brow, gasson".

There was that shiny glint in Paddy's left eye again. My antenna went up; there had to be a story here, most definitely. The foot tapping had begun. Paddy crossed his left leg over his right knee. His corduroy trouser leg was glazed, glazed with the friction of three-day old newspaper ink, moistened with rain and tobacco waste and laminated with pen-knife sharpening.

Of course, there will be a story here soon, wait till the oil tankers pass, and the loads of live fattened pigs. The rain would soon wash away the spills from the livestock trailers as they rounded the Billiard Room Corner.

"Can't figure it out, avick?" Paddy's eyes were glazed with mischief. "No problem. Ye wouldn't be the first one to be puzzled by that secret code, gasson. Mind ye, there was no flies on the boyos that invented our code of transporting messages.

"I'll just tell ye this much. There's a bunch of strangers wandering round South Armagh, now, as we spake at the present time, I think they are kinda homeless …I know they are penniless, anyway. They lead a sort of largely vagrant kinda life, gasson, spending usually about four months of the year around the hills of South Armagh, and they lie out at night, avick, within ould barns ate'n food out of rusty ould tins. They are a bit of a nuisance to local farmers cause sometimes there does be bits of fires started in the barns. Do ye know what I mane, gasson? And sometimes dacent peoples' property can get vandalized. They think nothing of putting their boot through a persons' front dure".

# Armagh-geddon

Paddy shifted his position from his 'Stone of Scone', as he called his Barrack Corner seat. It was Friday, Market day, and crowds were gathering. Paddy held the piebald foal by the mane while Tom Hughes, a renowned horse dealer from Crossmaglen, tied his bootlace.

"*Ducit Amor Patriae,*" he said repeatedly. He was back on his throne again. "At least this one is in its rightful place, gasson, not like the other 'Stone of Scone' they stole from Tara.

"Where was I, avick? *Ducit Amor Patriae* (love of country leads me). In Revelations 16:16 of the Good Book there's talk about a prophecy of a battle between the forces of good and evil at the end of the world. The scholarly trio from Shorts Lane, which is located midway down North Street in Crossmaglen and runs all the way to the Newry road, towel me that there was an ould Hebrew word – or maybe there's two words, avick; am not too sharp in those avenues, gasson – the words were Har Megiddo and that meant a hill at Megiddo."

Paddy went on to elaborate his knowledge of geography by stating that Megiddo was a big city twenty miles north of Samaria in the valley by the name of Kishon on the southern side of the Plain of Esdraelon somewhere in Palestine.

"The name of the place was Armageddon and it was the symbol of conflict. Teddy Roosevelt made mention of this famous place at a convention in Chicago when he shouted, 'We stood at Armageddon, and we battle for the Lord.' Be that as it may, gasson, that was 1912 and this is 1971 and be the stool am sitting on with the three legs under it, we're standing at Armagh-geddon and we're battling for Cross."

"It was round about or somewhere in between the year 1093 and 1096 that a pope be the name of Urban the second, called a council in the south of France. This was shortly after the Turks attacked Jerusalem, gasson. The pope towel his men to go out and take back the Holy Sepulchre from the infidels. That was the beginning of the problem we're encountering here today, that's what started Crossmaglen – the French crowd were using the Latin noun Crux. They started to call it 'Croisee' and then the English gobshites started to refer to it as "The Crux of the matter. Did ye ever hear the batin of it, avick? Then the Spanish and the French got a howlt of our name. The next thing was a boyo by the name of Johnson invented a word called "Croisade" in 1755 and the next thing that happened, gasson, was Noah Webster put it into the dictionary in 1828. The reason he was so anxious to include our town in his big book, was because no less a man than Thomas Jefferson wrote about us in 1786 when he towel them to 'preach, my dear sirs, a croisade against ignorance'.

"The English took the lend of 'Crosse' because they viewed it as a puzzling or difficult problem, and they wanted it to be described as in 'the crux of a problem', but let me tell you something, avick, and yer nobody's fool, check it out for yourself, gasson. The English could only invent the word 'Cross' by taking the original word 'Crux' from the ould Irish language, gasson. Whether or which, avick, it still represents the same today as it always did—crux – croisade – crusade – Cross—torture, from the 11th century till the 17th till the 21st, the more things change, the more they remain the same."

He was whistling now – and then he began humming a tune.

*"Oh, me name hadn't mattered for years,*
*And there's them that refused it reveres*
*Her few acres, you see, I fought hard to free*
*But in Cappy 'tis there I'll be free.*

*And 'tis oft times I think about Cappy*
*And the 'Baywin' and 'Kirks' garden, too*
*Though I'm not seen around*
*There my heart will be found*
*And it's Cappy to you I'll be true.*

*And the friends there so loyal and true*
*What an offer was made me and you*
*her rocks they are jagged*
*right there in the haggard*
*and her bogs they hold onto her dew.*

*Then again I can think of the Hauckney's*
*tucked there beneath ould Pete's Hill*
*if those friends could come back*
*there'd be piles of ould craic*
*all fuelled by the stroke of the quill.*

*Now I wander on over to Georgie's*
*And it's there that I'll split the breeze*
*From memories long gone*
*I'll sing this ould song cause in Cappy*
*It'sthere I will please*

*And it's oft times I think about Cappy*
*And the Baywin and Kirk's garden too*
*Though I'm not seen around*
*There my heart will be found*
*and it's Cappy to you I'll be true.*

(Pat Mc Entegart)

I allowed my gaze to wander along the concrete footpath at the Barrack Corner. While Paddy lilted his ballad, I began to notice many more indentations in the form of peculiar symbols, all around the surface closest to the curb. What did they signify? Tom trotted the piebald pony past us in a southerly direction.

"Ho, boy. Trot him over and walk him back. Ho, boy. Ho, boys, gasson."

Just then I remembered the call used by the mail handlers when delivering mail in the US. It was my grandad who told me that back in the 1880s "ho boy" was their call. Grandad also told me they had a series of secret symbols, a kind of survival kit.

Paddy eyed me mischievously. Hmm, what could it all mean? Basket-weave patterns in concrete with the letters 'n' and 'g' to their left and right on the Cullovile road side, pointed due south. I could clearly make out the formation of what looked to be an oblong or elongated o-ring with a plus sign at its north and south ends.

Paddy must have taken pity of my plight at this point, because he broke his silence by saying, "There will be no Hobson's choice round these parts today."

Thomas Hobson was a deliveryman back in 1631 who had a practice of requiring every customer to take the horse which stood nearest the door.

"This boyo taught the English this trick of forcing an apparent freedom to take or reject something when in actual fact no freedom exists," Paddy explained. "An apparent freedom of choice where in fact no freedom exists, gasson! Where there is no real alternative! Pon me sowel. No Hobson's choice.".

I was busy writing away. After all, there wasn't much else for me to do. I couldn't ask questions; well, there was no point, so I just kept on writing in between interruptions, which were frequent and very diversified. I was beginning to feel like how Giotto, the designer of the lower two storeys of the fourteenth century cathedral in Florence, must have felt, and I'm quite sure that Talenti, the designer of the next five stories, must have had pangs similar to those that I was experiencing, at the opening of the fifteenth century (such were the skills of building then).

No one in Florence had the faintest idea how the huge, octagonal central space of the semi-domes surrounded by the exterior masses of the nave was going to be covered. How would it be roofed? When would it be finished? Talenti's question was fast becoming juxtaposed with my own train of thought just then at the Barrack Corner in Crossmaglen as I tried hard to capture the correct essence of Paddy's mind set.

My plight was increased due mainly to the fact that I couldn't see a way in which I could delay the culmination of events around Crossmaglen in anticipation of 21$^{st}$ century relief in finishing this book, so I just kept on writing. I slowly became resigned to my own unwritten rule which, loosely stated, can be construed to represent the conclusion that this book will perhaps never be finished, or to put it another way, there will always be a recurring Crossmaglen story, "thank God".

"Ye tell me you're going to set up camp in Wrights Lane," Paddy said as he took stock of my shoulder bag. Wright's Lane is located one mile east of Crossmaglen on the Monoug road. "You'll not be lonesome, avick. There's plenty of boyos with rucksacks round these parts, gasson."

I was anxious to learn about the significance of this heather bank location with its chestnut tree-lined avenue that my Dad had described as my surveillance camp.

"You'll be treading in the footsteps of the poets Art McCooy and Padar O'Doran and McAlinden," he'd said. "It's important that you pitch tent according to the special instructions Paddy shall outline for you."

I was to walk out the Monog road beyond the base of Gaffney's Brae, into the valley of the Pigs Dyke. There I would see Drumuck Hill on my right. I was to enter the boreen on my left at the beginning of a demising forest. I would then be in the Vale of Creggan, which was once known as Dunreavy Wood. If I watched carefully at the correct time each morning, I would see the rising sun syphon the dew off the heather and transport it through the great gable on Wright's Barn en route to Creggan.

"So ye came to Cross lucking for work, gasson." Paddy eyed me up and down and across a couple of times.

"You got it, Paddy, that's my mission."

"mmmmuh aah I see there must be a bit of an Oriental strain in ye, avick. Sit down there on that other stool for a while till we have the craic."

"Craic" (pronounced krack) is a term for news, gossip, fun, entertainment and enjoyable conversation, particularly prominent in Ireland. The expression, "What's the craic?" means How are you? or What's happening? The word has an unusual history; the English *craic* was borrowed into Irish as *craic* in the mid-20th century and the Irish spelling was then re-borrowed into English. Under another spelling, the term has great cultural currency and significance in Ireland. (Source: Wikipedia, the free encyclopaedia.)

What was this? Illegal substances in Crossmaglen in the Seventies?

"No, Paddy," I protested. "Furthermore I never touch the stuff."

"Aahh, howl yer whisht, gasson, sure I know it's a new word in your American vocabulary, but we've been having the ould craic here for centuries."

I could see right away this town was different, but how different? Would I be able to find work? How much would I get paid? What would be my most gainful source of employment?

As I considered these questions, I took stock of the seat where Paddy sat. The taxi driver had earlier told me it was known as Paddy's "Stone of Scone". This remark had undoubtedly something to do with the misplaced stone in London that was forcibly removed from Tara Hill in Meath some centuries ago. My analysis of Paddy's Barrack Corner seat (which was a windowsill in the stone Barrack Corner building, was quickly interrupted by a brown rainbow of skilfully articulated spit from Paddy in tobacco formation, whose radius extended ten feet beyond me.

"Pon me sowel, avick, the only difference between this stone and the one in London is that this one is in its rightful place, and I only hope and pray that England is forced to put back the other stone in its rightful place on Tara Hill, gasson."

I gazed at Paddy, silently watching him breastfeed the top end of a hazel rod tucked in between his legs while he sat. Availing of the street light which shone above him, he firmly but gently held the rod with both hands close to his left-hand waistcoat pocket next to his chest. What did my father know in sending me to this town?

Paddy had read my thoughts just as clearly as if I had spoken them. My eyes were fixed upon the three, upended spiders drowning; they were located at the eastern end of Paddy's brown rainbow. What had I stumbled into? I suddenly began to wonder if the spiders had maybe flown in from a neighbouring island in the Atlantic. There was at least a half ounce of tobacco particles (not to mention the liquid lubricants) engulfing the stunned spiders; they were doomed. Did Paddy perhaps perceive them as being some other form of species not spiders? I soon realized how quickly my mind found work in Crossmaglen. What was this town like?

I looked away from the roadside carnage; they were beyond rescue. "Just like Boston, gasson, just like Boston."

I wondered what a market town in South Armagh could have in common with Boston. Somehow, I was getting the feeling that my life would never be the same again – never. Where was Paddy going with this line of thought, I wondered. Well let me see; where will I start?

Paddy was gazing north across the vast commons of Cross Square.

"Pauderdeen, my great grandfather, always maintained it was similar in size and supported the same usage as Boston Common in Colonial times. There was a boyo be the name of Shales who stubbed the whins on Cross Square, and he used to graze cows and goats on it. I was recalling having heard of Boston Commons been used to herd cows in Colonial times when Paddy drew my attention to the bottom of Cross Square to my left from where I stood at the Barrack Corner. In the Square's most northerly point stood a large, yellow, two-storey stone structure with a stone-slated roof and a commanding Doric palladium front porch, and overshadowing this building from its rear, stood a giant sycamore tree.

"There's another building of a similar type in that same garden, gasson, at a lower elevation, and it used to be known as McCormick's Loft. In me father's time," Paddy told me, "it was the Sinn Fein offices, during the 1916-1918 period. The outline of this building was deemed by historians as being similar to the Green Dragon Tavern in Boston, avick."

Paddy was towel as a child that it's within the Green Dragon that the Sons of Liberty planned the American Revolution and the famous "tay party", as Paddy described it.

"Are ye writin any of this down, avick? Ye were looking for work, isn't that what I heard ye saying?"

I had my tape recorder running as soon as I realized the wealth of knowledge Paddy had in store for me. Somehow the calmness of my Dad's confidence in placing his wager was beginning to unfold; there would be more, lots more to come.

Paddy was pointing across to McCusker's barber shop roof now.

"That's St Patrick's belfry and spire, gasson," he said. It was directly north of the local courthouse belfry and clock. "Pauderdeen towel me grandfather that there's a church just like our St Patrick's over in Boston, gasson, an he said it was known as the Old North Church. Would ye happen to know anything about that, avick?"

Paddy was getting all fired up now; there was nothing to be gained by interrupting his line of thought.

"I'll tell ye better than that, gasson. When I was a slip of a gasson meself, not the height of two pence of coppers, I heard my grandfather relating the craic about the boyos in Boston the night of April 18th 1775, and that's not today or yesterday, avick.

"Them boyos had a signal worked out that night, where one of them hung a lantern light in the belfry of the steeple to warn everyone about the approaching British army. Didn't that bate the divil for a plan and a half?"

I was conjuring up images of my dad's smiling face back in New York, and thinking that if I was going to keep a totally honest record of all my job opportunities and their time of commencement in Crossmaglen, then I'd better begin that record now.

> **Employer's name:** Paddy.
> **Nature of employment:** Swap-work.
> **Employee duties:** To offset Paddy's assumed handicap in reading and writing.
> **Time employment commenced:** August 29th 1971
> **When was employment commenced?** Instantly
> **Projected or forecasted salary anticipated:** Untold millions.

Paddy was availing of my pre-occupation with filling in these details. That's the way Paddy is: pragmatic. I noticed he was wrapping his tobacco chew in a separate handkerchief which appeared to be reserved for this purpose. He deposited this in the left-hand pocket of his gaberdine overcoat while at the same time he extracted a crumpled pack of Woodbine cigarettes from within the right-hand pocket of his waistcoat.

"Did ye take note of the front of McConville's House, gasson?" he asked as he lit his Woodbine from the flaming match he had just struck across the sole of his Shamrock-brand boot.

"There's a row of cobbled floor stables down that yard and there's men in this town would tell ye that Paul Revere's famous horse ride rose less sweat than was seen on the horses that left them stables. I'll tell ye better than that: there were tay chests down below there in the ould bakery that was far heavier than any that was thrown overboard at Griffen Warft."

Both of us now fixed our gaze upon the Ould Courthouse, as Paddy described it. "Since the launching of the Civil Rights Campaign here a couple of years ago, it has become known as Crossmaglen's Faneuil Hall".

Just then I could hear my Dad's warning in the back of my mind regarding the asking of questions, so I hesitated. Patience was the key. I began to look more closely at the structural layout of the local courthouse, or market house, roof, as Paddy described it, depending on the mood or frame of mind he was in. I noticed that the third-floor belfry was supporting the national tri-colour flag. That seemed okay to me as an Irish American, but I couldn't make the connection with Boston's Cradle of Liberty.

"The way it is here, avick. According to the forces of foreign rule in these parts, Crossmaglen been one of the chief marketing towns in the one fair county of Ireland, we are forbidden to fly our national emblem.

"Pauderdeen always maintained that in Colonial times the retired sailors of Boston were prone to lashing a keg of whiskey to their rocking chairs in the foyer of Fanueil Hall to imitate the rolling motion of the sailing ships which gave their whiskey a better flavour."

At this point it's only fair to enlighten readers as to the various peculiarities and mannerisms Paddy would have inherited from his ancient Celtic ancestors, not least of which is the custom of flavouring the visitor's cup of tea ("tay") with an undisclosed amount of whiskey. The rationale behind this custom was based on the theory that the fusion of caffeine and whiskey would ignite modulations of voluntary hypnosis within the unsuspecting traveller to Crossmaglen.

"The practise was always assured to eliminate all resistance to price changes in open market dalin in horses, pigs, cattle, goats, tin cans, duck eggs, bald roosters, cantankerous women and disgruntled bachelors," Paddy explained. There was even a famous song written about it:

*Shure it wa'nt the boys from Keady*
*Nor the lads from Ballybay*
*'Twas Johnny Coy the tricky boy*
*Put the whiskey in me tay.*

"Are you finding yer bearings, avick?"

Paddy's voice contained a note of laughter and his face was brandishing a broad smile. I drank a cup of Irish tea once; my Mother had bought it from the Irish store in the Bronx. "There's history in that tea, son," my Dad had said, "lots of history. You need to go there and hear it from the people at grassroots level."

Well, I was here now in Crossmaglen, and I was remembering extracts from a book I had studied entitled *Natural History*, written by Arthur Marwick. (The word "history" in English comes from the Greek word "historia" which meant to inquire, but in the German, "Geschichte" means what happened. "We cannot know what happened if we do not first inquire into a given event."

Then there were the comments from the Open University course A101, Unit 3, Intro to History, which suggested that if you look around you at houses, buildings, churches etc., immediately you are involved in some kind of historical contact with the past from which these buildings originated. Even if you ignore all this, even if we look blindly at the buildings around us and never indulge in any serious conversation about their origins, nonetheless, whether we like it or not, much of what happens to us in our lives is governed by developments which took place in the past, or sometimes what people thought happened in the past.

Arthur Marwick makes the point, that no society can get along without knowledge of its history. Some might not agree with him, but where would we be without memory? A community suffering from loss of memory is in a very tricky situation; it will always have difficulty in adjusting itself to other communities, in finding its bearings. "In making intelligent decisions about itself, it has lost its sense of identity. The question is often asked, what is history? And if you employ a South Armagh tactic in answering that question, then you would be turning the tables round on the questioner by suggesting that they "try to imagine what it would be like living in a society where there was no knowledge whatsoever of history".

"I see you're getting settled into your work rightly, avick", Paddy observed.

"Yes," I replied, "I feel I'm getting a bit more orientated. I'm beginning to establish a sense of identity."

"In other words, yer finding yer bearings, gasson."

My dad had prepared me admirably in all aspects of how I was to conduct my stay in Crossmaglen. He had drawn a line down the centre of a page so as to make an impression on my mind regarding do's and don'ts. He used a red marker to drive home his point. I can see the first "don't" to this day: "Don't ask questions, at least not directly."

You'll need to be creative, he continued. Approach matters in a seemingly uninterested frame of mind, be patient, engage in small talk, but be aware always that the boys and girls around Crossmaglen can read your mind for you. We call it cutting a bush to bate yourself.

Paddy said, right on cue, without batting an eyelid, had I a job on my hands?

> Was there an abundance of work for me in Crossmaglen?
> How many would I need on my research team?
> Was Paddy an historian?
> How long did the retired sailors rock their whiskey kegs for?
> Was there a connection between the Fane in Faneuil Hall and the Fane River in South Armagh?
> How would I discover the significance of Paddy's reference to the Brewer's Kegs?
> Why did Paddy place the newspaper upside down on his lap as he sat in his appointed position?

These and many more questions were flowing through my mind as I tried to ascertain a method of approach in unearthing the characteristics of Crossmaglen, South Armagh, Ireland.

I knew that Bushmills in County Antrim was the oldest distillery in the world and that they still used heavy wood casks to ferment their whiskey. I remembered hearing my grandfather describe the autumn berry picking season during the harvesting time in South Armagh each year. He'd said the earnings from the berries went towards purchasing new footwear and clothing for the back-to-school season. It was during one of these experiences that my grandfather received instructions from Kate Keenan, an elderly lady from Cappy, on the art of primitive wine fermentation.

Kate instructed my granddad, who was a child at the time, to fill some glass jam-jars with berries and then to bury them beneath the ground in the peat moss of Cappy in the Baroney of the Fews. Kate said this process would produce wine of a quality that would knock the socks off the strongest of travellers who were unaccustomed to the ways of South Armagh.

"You see, gasson," Paddy was saying, "there's them that would tell you to this day that the Irish monks got their inspiration for the ancient love knot of Ireland right here in the Barony of the Fews in Crossmaglen, South Armagh. Now, where was I with me craic about who is copying who? I wanted to tell you about my cattle smuggling drives across Mulligan's Cais."

Mulligan's Cais (pronounced 'Kesh') is a small wooden footbridge which straddles the border stream between the counties Armagh and Louth in the townlands of Mobane and Courtbane.

"I'll get back to that one later, gasson. Sure they accuse us of been backward here in Cross and they be inclined to make fun of us just because we project an image of belonging to the past, but maybe them same folk have no past of their own.

"Let's suppose someone comes along and confiscates all yer bits of belongings and begins to tell you what you can and cannot do or say. Let's take it a bit further, gasson. How would it be if they forced you to stop what you were engaged in and insisted on you doing something totally foreign to yerself, like spaking their language which is absolutely inferior to yer own native tongue.

"Yer a well-travelled young student an am going to suggest to you that after all that 'supposed' interference in your private life, you were determined to hold on to your sense of identity that we talked about earlier, gasson. You would have to look back beyond the interruption to recollect your thoughts and plans and prepare for the future – an in order to make any kind of sense of the present.

"Uh uh. Where was I, anyway, with me other craic? Pon me sowel, there's that much stuff in me ould head that sometimes it gets jammed up, avick, do you know what I mane, gasson? I have it now: Mulligan's Cais. It was a link road to the Free State, to Meath of the Pastures. Kind of what these boyos round here would call an unapproved border crossing.

"The smugglers, or the dalin men, had set up this link road between Cross and Meath on a monthly basis back in the early Fifties. I was only a slip of a gasson meself then. We used to be hearing a lot of talk coming out of a wet battery radio in PA Murphy's garage in Cross. It used to spit out cracks and farts at us coming from school. There was a man's voice telling us about the students in Budapest, Hungary, tackling the Russian armoured tanks with their bare hands, and he said that the people of Budapest were forced to flee for their lives across a small wooden bridge known as the Bridge of Andau."

"That's a new one on me, Paddy" I said.

"It's just like Mulligan's Cais, avick. Howel on there a minute – I was started to tell you about the Ancient Love Knot there a while ago, didn't I?"

"Yes, Paddy."

"I began to say how it was believed locally that the monks obtained their inspiration for its design in and around the Crossmaglen area. Oh yes, correct, gasson, that was during the time of all the chaos in Europe.

"According to the stories I heard, it was after the fall of the Roman Empire. All the art treasures of Ireland were been plundered by vandals. Could ye bate that, avick? The monks of Ireland who were residing in some of the great monasteries up there in Louth and in Bangor and Armagh travelled inland to the ancient castle of the O'Nales of Glassdrumman outside Crossmaglen and the round tower in Inniskeen."

"Look round you, gasson. You're surrounded by ancient forts, and some not so ancient."

"Ah," I said.

"Yer nobody's fool, avick, but getting back to me, craic. You work this one out yourself, gasson. You're sitting here in the middle of the Armagh Drumlins with rolling hillside all around you. There's Creevekeeran to your west, Drumuckavall to your east and Carron to the north. That's what the ancient monks plotted on their canvas when they stood in the middle of Cross Square, gasson. When the monks had their continuous unbroken line weaved through and around Cross, they noticed the ring forts of Corliss and Lissaraw together with the Batine Mor in between the other vantage points outside.

"It was commonly understood by the descendants of those monks that the vertical axis line plotted west from Creevekeeran through Cross to O'Nale's Castle site in the east, in devotion to the rising sun. The monks then symbolically threw a gold ribbon around the three outer extremes of their configuration, and entwined Crossmaglen in the centre by enclosing it within the Gold Ring of Fidelity. But let me tell you, avick, it's not everyone in these parts that has that quality of a belief system. I have a sort of a notion, gasson, that some of them might still be suffering from the king's evil."

This was another of Paddy's diversions that my Dad had warned me to look out for; these off-the-cuff remarks or renditions appeared to exude from him more readily while he was engaged in his tobacco-chewing hobby.

"Sounds like some sort of debauchery from olden days, Paddy, that King's Evil thing. Maybe a Cromwellian proclamation."

"Well, gasson, there's a glimmer of hope for you yet in these rolling hills and shady valleys. I hope your father is well versed in the biblical story, the one about turning your money over and over without giving away too much of a luck-penny to the other fellow. Don't worry too much about your father; keep your mind on your work here in Cross and if your father's stuck for ideas as to what to do with his winnings from the wager he placed on your coming to Cross, there's plenty of boyo's around here that will tell him what kind of fuel to purchase that will make him rich."

Where was I, gasson, with me craic? Oh yeh – the King's Evil. Man's sowel, but it was a blaggard of a disease back in the middle ages. Scrofula was the proper medical term for it, and it was rampant until well into the 19$^{th}$ century, affecting sufferers with glandular swellings of a very painful nature.

It's a funny thing about ould cures, like for example the custom round these parts of rubbing a live snail across the warts on a child's hand and then pinning the unfortunate snail to a gooseberry bush. People believed that when the snail died, the warts would also die. They believed that the snail had some sort of power over the child's skin. They were in some cases proved correct; the only time that failure was reported was whenever the child refused to believe in the snail's power to influence the end result.

Paddy himself had many times exercised a positive belief in the harmonious results of certain tough cases of illness, and a strong belief that he could improve his own lot and the circumstances of others, without resorting to the unnecessary tanning of snail hides on goose-berry bushes.

"But where were we ladin up to with me ould craic, gasson?" Paddy took off his cap and scratched his head; it was Woodbine time again. "So it's work yer looking for, avick, isn't that what I heard you saying? Hu-well, if you can help me straighten out all that's under this ould cap of mine, you will not have many an idle day or night, gasson. Now I'm not forgetting about Mulligan's Kesh, divil the fear of that, gasson. We'll cross that Andau Bridge when we come to it.

"Right, me flower, I have it now – the King's Evil. The cure was, surprisingly enough, very simple, gasson. All the sufferer had to do was to petition an anointed sovereign to touch the diseased area of the patient – pon me sowel, are you listening carefully to what I'm saying, gasson? – these poor unfortunates were brainwashed into believing that an ordinary human like ourselves (only better fed), with a bit of dacent clothes and a metal hat made of pewther on their head, had the power to decide whether the patient lived or died!"

Paddy made the sign of the Cross on his chest. At the same time, he let fly one of his radial tobacco spits in the direction of Corliss Fort, with the ensuing result that its contents were responsible for ending a vicious battle between two stray dogs adjacent to the local butcher's shop door.

"Belief in the healing power of crowned royalty was so widely accepted in them days that the kings of England and France had to set aside certain days of the year when those affected by the scrofula could come to be cured. Could ye bate that, gasson? Charles the Second lent his so-called healing power to 90,000 of his subjects and Queen Anne was freely administering her cures to hundreds of people, including a boyo by the name of Samuel Johnston who was supposed to be touched as a child."

If I was looking for some overtime in my work assignment in Cross, I could do myself a favour by doing a bit of research into that name, Johnston.

Dean Jonathan Swift made very similar comments in the 1740s. He was a constant visitor to Gosford Castle outside Markethill, which is where he wrote *Gulliver's Travels*. Swift also wrote of his fear of the Tories he might meet as he made his way from Dundalk through Silverbridge and Dorsey and on by Ballymoyer to Markethill. And that was with the protection of the most feared Tory-hunter of them all, John Johnston – Johnston of the Fews – who claimed to have beheaded over a hundred bandits. Well, he didn't do his own beheading; he left that job to a turncoat called Owen Keenan from Tullyvallen. In Dorsey, not far from the big house that Johnston called Roxborough after the village his people came from in Scotland, there is a bog called the Tory Hole. Maybe we should dredge it for skulls. The man in question is John Johnston feared Tory- Hunter.

https://sites.google.com/site/gapothenorth/gap-o-the-north-walking-club/we-were-a-tory-stronghold

"There was a boyo by that name up there in them hills beyond Monog there, gasson, a few centuries ago, and mind you the people of Cross will not forget him. There was a prayer composed about him. 'Jesus of Nazereth, king of the Jews, save us from Johnston, king of the Fews.' Well that's another craic for some wet day we haven't much to do and I'm not too sure how much work you can cope with, gasson."

Paddy stopped abruptly to light another Woodbine.

"Do you know what I'm going to tell you, avick? You're going to need help, pon me sowel, lots of help,'cause I'll tell you why and this is a candid fact, gasson, as sure as you're standing here at the Barrack Corner in Cross.

"It will take a lot of time and effort to calculate the full extent of the damage done by them so-called anointed monarchs down through the ages till the present time. If I could manage to weave some sort of a global web from where you're standing that could begin to calculate the pain that was and still is been caused by persons in authority who continue to wield their authority as a weapon for suppressing the truth, just as those wealth-appointed, jewel-bedecked rulers of peasants had taken it upon themselves to claim divine teaching as their own private property.

"If only the people of the Dark Ages had been properly informed about the story of the lady with the issue of blood who hung around the outskirts of the large crowds waiting her chance to touch her Makers' cloak. Those people were nobody's fools. If they had heard the lady's reply to Our Lord's question—'Do you believe, ma'am, that I can do this for you?' 'Yes, Lord,' she said, 'I believe.' Then it is done unto you according to how you believe. Then there would be far less homage paid to earthly grabbers of people's minds."

"The corrupt rulers of them times misused the teaching that had been giving them, they suppressed the truth and used it for their own personal gain. Their purpose was to gain control of their subjects. It wasn't until somehow or someone later managed to put James the First on some sort of guilt trip, most likely himself, that the common people were allowed to read about the one thing over which they have total control in this life, that is the thoughts you allow into your mind."

"It is done onto you according to how you believe, not what some worn-out member of a dysfunctional family who has not paid their taxes decides will be done onto you. Now I'll get back to Mulligan's Kesh, but don't forget what I towel you about the lingering effects of that ould belief system from the Middle Ages. Before people heard the true word of God in certain parts of this earth, the harm was done by false gods. We were warned about them in His teaching. And I'll tell you something right now, gasson, we're takin a batin here in Cross at this minute right now as I spake from those descendants of the former coercers of truth, gasson."

It was drowning time again only this time it was the roadside cast-iron grating that received the last dregs of Paddy's Carroll's Number 1 tobacco ounce. That "It'll be back in Dundalk in a week where it came from, but it will have to pass under Mulligan's Kesh" first Paddy said. Talking with Paddy was like mixing vegetable soup in a large pot: You know the ingredients are all in the pot and they smell delicious, but as soon as you stop stirring the best ones settle to the bottom. Or maybe it was a bit like fishing with a bad rod or a weak line, or worse still, with the wrong bait, which invites only small nibbles and leaves you cursing your luck.

Whatever it was I was experiencing at that moment in Crossmaglen, I was beginning to see that it required an expertise that I was lacking to draw the big fish out of Paddy's reservoir of knowledge. Right then I was feeling like a one-armed paper hanger in a windstorm, but I was learning, or at least, I was trying to learn, and if nothing better, I had found work. But this Andau Bridge; how was I going to get Paddy back to Mulligan's Kesh?

Henry Ford said thinking was the hardest work one could do. He also said that is why so few engage in it.

It was Paddy who came to my rescue. "Where were we, gasson?" he asked. "We covered a lot of ground there." He was on his second pack of Woodbine now. "Let me see now. Yeah, we talked about figuring out where it all started, gasson, then I started to tell you about the mass pads and the smuggling exploits through Lissaraw Street, gasson. What year was that?

"Let me see. Armagh got to the All-Ireland in '53. I was there that day, gasson, and they would have won, too, if they had of put Kevin O'Callaghan on in the second half. I can still see him warming up on the side-line. The Meath men weren't slow, either, when I come to think about it; they had the biggest lumps of cattle that ever were seen, and you know what they used to do, gasson? They would drive them to Ardee Fair in County Louth cause they knew that Cross Fair was on the next day and prices were higher in the north.

"The southern boys had a bit of a problem: They didn't have the location of the movable bridge at Mulligan's. The Longford men had the same problem, and the Cavan boys were in the same boat, so they would drive as far as Carrickmacross or Ballybay. The sights that were seen on Cross Square just out where you're gazing now, gasson, left many an RUC policeman (Royal Ulster Constabulary) with high blood-pressure. There were shorthorn bullocks as big as buffaloes coming onto the Square after their one-night stand on Cappy Rock. Ye know, gasson, there should be a monument raised in honour of the men that built our Andau Bridge in Mulligan's meadow."

Then Paddy switched his craic to John Roebling, who he said built the Brooklyn Bridge.

"He must have had a brilliant mind," I said.

"Well, I'll just tell you, gasson, Roebling was the son of a poor immigrant who understood fully what Henry Ford was on about. And when the problem surrounding Roebling took his life, his son Washington stepped into his father's shoes. It was a bit like yer man Tommy down the road at Keady who wote 'The Four Green Fields' – *their sons will have sons as brave as were their fathers.* And of course Makem was just after leaving Cross when he pulled onto the hard shoulder and wrote those words.

"But getting back to Roebling and the Brooklyn Bridge, you're right, gasson, the Roebling team were smart, but there was something else involved in their success.

"They say that behind every good man stands a good woman. When Washington Roebling became crippled from an accident below the waters of the Hudson River during an inspection of the underwater caissons, his dream of a bridge between people seemed doomed.

"For 14 years he could not move a muscle except to tap with the index finger on his right hand. Roebling's wife Emily became his eyes, ears, voice and feet. In the 14 years it took to build the Brooklyn Bridge, Emily taught herself engineering, negotiating, supervisory, and political skills, while her husband could merely watch his dream from across the river, Mrs Roebling built their bridge.

"There was women around South Armagh made of the same kind of stuff as Emily Roebling. There should be a monument built in recognition of their efforts to build bridges to other communities. One side of the monument could be dedicated to the bridges of misrepresentation which these women tore down with their bare hands.

"Where were we, gasson? We strayed a long way from Mulligan's Kesh there. Again it's Sam's Lonin when I was a slip of a gasson, Sam's Lonin was the route we took every first Thursday of the month. We crossed the stone stiles, up through the Still House, down through Lissaraw Street, over across the boundary drain between Cappy and Lissaraw, onto Feeney's Lane to McCoy's football field in Mobane. That field tested the sprinting ability of a lot of Free State cattle 'cause it spanned the only 100-yard section of public roadway on the entire route. We then hung a quick left into Biddy Phil's Lonin (Bridget McCoy) at the Two Shilling Bits (Mick Burns') cottage, up through Kenny's (McCoy) street and onto Mulligan's Kesh.

"The square of Crossmaglen is a rectangle so therefore the sum of no other two sides anywhere in this world can be equal till it."

# Paddy's medicine for the "sowel", or, the Bible according to Paddy: quotes mixed with tobacco to chew on

"When we ask, we do not receive because we ask with Cross motives and we ask with right motives, but they'd rather spend what they keep from us on their own pleasures." Wee Jamsie, 35-37.

"Crossmaglen has no problems – only Copabilities and Capabilities." Patrick J McEntegart.

Paddy foils the plan of foreign nations, he upends the purposes of the strangers, but the plans of Paddy are floating in the world on the winds that blow around the Barrack Corner in Crossmaglen and they settle firmly there forever, the purposes of Paddy's heart for future generations." Paddy's left palm, 30-01-71.

## The spider and her web

"There's too much talk about the fact we can do nothing without foreign funding, but them that believe in themselves could renew their strength. They could start by imitating the spider building her web; they could let their ideas and inventions fly all over the world, and they'd be able then to run. They'd never be weary, and they'd be walking tall, too, and they'd never again faint with the hunger." John Peter with Jamsie at Luke's Corner one fair day.

## Crossmaglen University

"Crossmaglen has the largest open-air university in the world. It's not that easy to locate on your regular map due mainly to the fact that it's not on any map ever printed. Its main entrance is through a tunnel somewhere beneath a big, big house on the Cullovile road, close to the Barrack Corner. Its faculty is forever being rotated with the seasons of the year. This establishment is known all over the world for its generous distribution of PhD certificates," including the one conferred on Paddy himself at the Barrack Corner, which he said represented his achievement in Poverty, Hunger and Depression.

42

"Several eejits have counted the seeds in an apple, but find me the mathematician that could count the seeds in the ragworts and thistles that grows between the briars in South Armagh. Nowhere in Ireland or the whole world for that matter is there more desire for land than in Crossmaglen. According to Sherri Melsby, the most successful man is one who can lay a firm foundation with the bricks others throw at him. Well, bejazz--us it's a long road there's no turn on."

# Strangers in Crossmaglen

"Pon me sowel, there's a piece of land in Cross, gasson, that was a swamp full of bog-holes up until the natives started throwing stones and bricks at the big house on the Culloville Road back in 1969-70. The young folk got it into their heads that the paving slabs on the footpaths were not up to standard, so they ripped them up and fired them, too. The big house was sort of semi-derelict and it had been taken over by the strangers in the middle of the night.

"When all the dacent people were in their beds, the strangers would think nothing of working at tearing down walls and banging at big steel girders. They were thought to be pouring concrete all through the night 'cause there was women on the Eleven Row walking the flure all night with their young ones unable to sleep because of the racket created by the strangers.

"This community would never be the same again because of the disturbances. Pon me sowel, gasson, these strangers caused good, upstanding mothers' sons to partake of nightly measures of lubricants – purely for medicinal purposes, mind you. When the Sacred Heart Sodality (a church service) was disrupted, people took to open-air prayer vigils outside the big house" – the army barracks – "might as well be throwing chaff against the wind, gasson. Pure waste of time.

The strangers kept working during the night time, carting loads of brick and broken concrete out to the dump on the Culloville Road. They had that much rubble that they filled the dump up to road level and now it is a four-acre field of agriculture land.

"There comes a time in the long, wet evenings when all the praties were dug and the pits covered. Most of the farmers had milking machines and running water at the cow sheds. The Gaelic football season was drawing to a close. Irish dancing was performed mainly at weekends. The silage was organized on a self-feed basis, apart from locally built centres erected on a voluntary basis, and there was little or no amusement or recreation facilities for the youth of the community".

"They began to organize vigilante groups to deal with the strangers who were robbing them of much-needed sleep and causing their fathers and big brothers to become dependent on 'liquid sleeping remedies'.

"The youths started breaking up the paving slabs from the footpaths round the Barrack Corner. All the prayers didn't do any good. The youths were exhausted from lack of sleep; these strangers were banging at steel girders with 20-pound sledge hammers all night, every night.

"The town was at its wits' end. How would you like to go without sleep for weeks without end, gasson? The four acres of land out at the bog pass was made from steel beams and broken slabs of concrete that was fired at the strangers by the youths who were deprived of sleep by the racket that the strangers made in trying to make the big house liveable for themselves.

"It was all done by strangers in the night exchanging glances and local youths taking awful chances. There was a herd of Charlie cattle now grazing on what was previously a swamp, all started by the throwing of bricks and stones at the big house on the Culloville Road. It's a long road; there's no turn on it. Funny ould thing that, the way the strangers cut a bush to bate themselves.

"There was a boyo be the name of Corotius. He was supposed to be some sort of a British prince begging your pardon and all that, gasson. Could you bate that? There's them that would try to tell you – now this was back in the 5ᵗʰ century am talking about, gasson – this Corotius was supposed to be connected to a Welsh prince by the name of Ceredig. It bate all ever he heard and he heard manys a tall craic in his time.

"But I'll carry on with me craic anyway, gasson. If there's anything false about what am telling you, gasson, you can take your objections down through north street and hang a right into Shorts Lane, there will be a few scholarly boyos there that will straighten out any crevices and fill in the blanks for you, gasson.

"This Ceredig fella took over the strangers' ground after the Romans pulled out round about the year 400. Well, the bejas-an-us, and that's not today or yesterday. Yer man was some sort of a dacent Christian and he started to come to the aid of other Christians who were being attacked and abducted by pirates.

"There was one slip of a gasson a couple of years earlier who had been abducted and taken to Ireland. Didn't it bate the divil, gasson, that the gasson was carrying the same name as meself, avick! Some things never change. Where was I, gasson, with the British prince or was he the prince of Wales?"

He put this question to me as he stopped page five of *The Dundalk Democrat* from sliding along the street. It was been carried west past the British army post opposite the Barrack Corner by a gale-force wind. A trio of Paddy's tobacco spits thwarted the wind's efforts, and the newspaper stayed with us. Hay for sale, first cutting, baled without rain, can be delivered for one pound sterling per bale, punts ok.

I wondered how if it was made in Ireland, it could have been made without rain but who was I to question *The Dundalk Democrat*, especially when I was promptly informed by Paddy of the newspaper's close affinity with Cross.

"Read the Cross notes, gasson, especially the one that highlights the sufferings of the people of Cross in the Seventies. Where were we before *The Democrat* was delivered late? Made no odds to meself, avick, if it never came. Can't make a trick of it.

"Yer man Ceredig was supposed to have been the one who invented the cardigan, could ye bate that, gasson? Either way or not, this boyo wielded a lot of clout over in the south of England, and it appears to me, avick, that he organized warring parties against the young Patrick that was sent to Ireland at the time.

"This fella Ceredig came over from England and when he discovered that Patrick had converted whole bunches of men to a more civilized way of doing things. What did the Ceredig fella do but begin to slaughter huge numbers of Patrick's new Christians? Pon me sowel, gasson, and you're standing here wondering what's wrong with Crossmaglen.

What do you make of it all, gasson? A Welsh prince Ceredig in the 5$^{th}$ century slaughtering innocent civilians and we have representatives of a Welsh prince here in this town at the minute who have slaughtered innocent civilians in. The bloody eejits damn the learning they got, they are digging in night and day, these boyo's are that fond of digging that they even dug up country roads to prevent the parishioners from attending mass in the Sacred Heart Church in Shelagh Co Louth..

"Are you sure you have enough lead in that pencil of yours to finish me craic, gasson? It's a holy terror, gasson, the way history repeats itself. Bates the divil them eejits in England can never learn anything. Ceredig gathered up all the Irish he couldn't slaughter and had them bonded into slavery. This boyo Ceredig wouldn't even accept a letter of protest from Patrick. Mind you, gasson, just because I can't write doesn't mane all the Patricks were struck with the same malady."

# Saint Patrick

According to my Shorts Lane fraternity, there was a brave strain on relations between Patrick and the British. Funny thing that, gasson, the way some things never change."

Paddy met one of the scholarly trio during one of his infrequent dry spells in Shorts Snug one night in North Street, Crossmaglen. The pub consists of a snug off the main bar at the rear with a side entrance on to Shorts Lane, adjoining North Street. Most of the customers were elderly farmers. Some of them wore hats, others wore caps; some smoked pipes while others chewed tobacco and would spit out occasionally as they told their stories of days gone by.

He took a letter from within the lining of his cap which he said he had got from his great grandfather Pauderdeen, who got it from a cousin of an uncle of a great grandson of the saint. Columbkille was his name. This letter was written in ould Gaelic. According to a friend of the schoolmaster, there was a man named Ludwig Bielen who was supposed to have translated it in the early 1950's. It was this schoolmaster that Paddy hoped to find when he went to Shorts Snug that night.

He and the went outside to moisten the ragworts – "to make it easier for the bees at their cross pollination", Paddy explained. When they had finished, the schoolmaster read Patrick's letter out loud for him.

> *I, Patrick, a sinner, unlearned, resident in Ireland, declare myself to be a bishop, and with my own hand I have written and composed these words to be given, delivered and sent to the soldiers of Britain.*
>
> *I live for my God to teach the heathens even though some of them may despise me, not that I wish my mouth to utter anything as hard and harsh, but I'm forced by the zeal of my maker and to tell you the truth. Christ has rung it from me . . . Out of love for my neighbours and sons for whom I gave up my country and parents and my life to the point of death.*

"*If I be worthy.* I'll use Patrick's words when he asked the British to return some of the booty and the baptized they had made captives. The British laughed at him." I do not know what to lament the most – those who have been slain or those who have been held captive, or those who the devil has befriended.

"Pon me sowel, gasson, but it had a powerful ring of truth about it! I'll just tell you, 15 or 16 centuries later there's not much that has changed. *Wherefore let all God-fearing men know they are also enemies of me.* Pon me sowel, Patrick had a bit of a temper, like meself!"

Parricide, fratricide, 'ravening wolves that ate people of the Lord as they ate bread', as Patrick put it,

> *the wicked Lord have destroyed thy law which, but recently, he had excellently and kindly planted in Ireland. I make no false claim, I share in the work of those who preach the gospel amid grave persecutions unto the end of the earth.*
>
> *Wherefore then I plead with you earnestly, ye holy and humble of heart, it is not permissible to court the favour of such people nor to take food or drink with them, nor even to accept alms until they make reparations to God in hardships through penance with shedding tears, and set free the baptised servants of Christ for whom He died and was crucified.*

"Pon me sowel, gasson," Paddy exclaimed, "it was all starting to make sense to him just as I spake these words, gasson. I'll tell you about it later. Where was I? Pon me sowel, it would make your blood boil, gasson!"

> *The most high disapproveth the gifts of the wicked, he that offereth sacrifice of the goods of the poor is as one that sacrificeth the son in the presence of the father, it is written that the riches which he gathered unjustly shall be vomited up from his belly, the angel of death drags him away by the fury of dragons he shall be tormented.*

"Pon me sowel, gasson! 'I am Patrick a sinner, much unlearned, the least of all the faithful and utterly despised by many.' When I was sixteen year ould, I was taken into captivity in Ireland, with many thousands of my people, hence I cannot be silent nor indeed expedient about the great benefits and the great graces which the Lord has designed to bestow upon me in the land of my captivity. Although I am imperfect in many things, I nevertheless wish that my brethren and kinsmen should know what sort of person I am'."

## About Paddy

Paddy is 6 feet tall and of slim build. He lives in an old cottage which resembles a clay and wattle structure of the 19th century. The cottage is well maintained and has a half door in good repair, flagstone floors and a three-legged stool in front of his Doric cooker which shines with enamel polish. Occasionally a neighbour lady, Katie McEnteggart, and her husband Mickey come visiting and bake some cakes of bread for him.

Bread baking in Paddy's cottage

Paddy takes great pride in keeping his humble cottage spotless. He has an easy chair in front of the cooker in which he reflects on his current situation when thinking about the day that has just passed. He always wears a cap and tips it as a matter of curiosity when he meets his neighbours. He sometimes wears a worn tweed suit and other times wears one-piece gaberdine overalls. He wears Shamrock brand leather boots with steel toecaps and steel heels. The soles are riveted with nails, so you can hear him coming a long way off. Paddy is a bachelor and works as a casual labourer, often doing odd jobs that are poorly paid as a means to survive. Paddy is illiterate but possesses a keen mind. He was born in 1936 and he is now thirty-five years old with the wisdom of a sixty-year old and is keen to make his mark on the world.

During one particular visit, he confided in me that he sometimes felt that he couldn't escape a feeling of inferiority among people with regular employment, even though he knew they were definitely not his equal in character, intelligence or ability. These people – even his friends – -feel, on the other hand, a sense of superiority and regard him, perhaps unconsciously, as a casualty of life or a failure.

His whitewashed cottage is ornate and includes a small vegetable garden which he tends in the spring time. The garden is surrounded with an evergreen hedge and numerous trees.

There is no through road to his cottage. It is approached through numerous fields by a narrow boreen and his nearest neighbour lives a quarter mile away. That evening Paddy invited me to his cottage for some dinner. Paddy adjusted the notches on his broad black leather belt as he re-positioned his rush-caned chair back beneath the kitchen table with his right knee and busied himself with preparing the meal. He had potatoes ('spuds' or 'praties', as Paddy called them) in one saucepan, in another he had curly cabbage and carrots, while in a third he had boiling bacon. While all this was simmering he retrieved two large mugs from the dresser.

Then he went to the butter churn, filled the two mugs with buttermilk and placed them on the table.

"Boy, that's strong stuff, Paddy!" I observed.

"That'll put hairs on yer chest like barbed wire, gasson," he said as he got two plates and put them in the oven to warm.

Soon after that he was ready to serve dinner. As we ate, Paddy talked about old times around Cross and the journeymen and old tinkers calling at his cottage when he was a boy

"The journeymen would always be selling tay, gasson, and the tinker Davey Joyce would be asking for an ould pot to mend. Me mother would always invite them in for something to ate."

When dinner was finished Paddy stood up. "Thanks be to God for that feed. We are not sure of the next one," he said, making the sign of the cross on his chest.

As Paddy washed up after dinner I had a chance to take in my surroundings. To my right along the gable wall of the kitchen there stood a fine antique Irish dresser decked out with a full set of willow pattern delph. Along the opposite wall stood an antique settle bed which served as a rest spot for a weary traveller who might chance to stop by at night.

Further on there stood a wooden, end-over-end butter churn, and on the side wall was the sturdy kitchen table complete with footrest. Next to the table was an earthen crock that held the water from Paddy's spring well in the garden. Alongside the crock was a galvanized bath with a ribbed glass washing board.

Over the fireplace there hung a picture of the Sacred Heart with sprigs of palm jutting out from both sides at its base. As the bedroom door was open I could see Paddy's wrought iron bed, alongside of which was a small table with a large, Victorian bowl and jug for washing purposes. In the corner stood his armchair commode.

Paddy's cottage built in the 19th century

The floor of the cottage was made of earthen stone flags and as Paddy began to sweep them I took a stroll out into his front yard. Surrounding the yard to the east stood some small stone out-offices, the smallest one being a kennel for Emerald, Paddy's dog. Close to it stood a hen house for Paddy's Rhode Island Red hens, who supplied him with his daily supply of fresh free-range eggs.

There was another shed also which housed his Hercules bicycle and his firewood and meal for his collie dog. It was on his Hercules bicycle that Paddy often pushed a 100-lb. bag of maize meal (dog food) home across the fields from Crossmaglen, uphill and downhill, sometimes in the dark of night. All the out-offices were neatly whitewashed with a black tar plinth along their base. Around the front porch of the cottage there were arranged, in the shape of an arch, some rose bushes which I figured must be a beautiful sight when in full bloom in summertime.

"Bad scrant to them! Poor ould Cross, they tried to destroy us."

"Where was I, gasson? More mortar and wee stones as Joe McKenna said. Pon me sowel, the more things change, the more they remain the same. Funny ould thing that: the more weight you put on a small twig the more it will grow, and the more weight you put on the keystone in an arch the stronger it becomes."

Paddy was whistling now, and somehow I was beginning to recognize the air from an old tune I had heard my grandfather singing bits of. That's the way the Celts are – multi-layered activities juxtapose in their minds, all rolled into one timeframe, human thoughts seemingly hung out to dry on the wild flora of intellectual clotheslines, maintaining a fixation of contact with their Creator akin to professional fishers of men in bygone ages, shaking their heads with utterances of "Let it be" and "Thy will be done".

I was mentally composing my own caption beneath Paddy's stone of scone as he began singing what he had been whistling: *Catch me if you can, me name is Dan and I'm your man.* I thought how fitting it would be to erect just a small plaque in this spot that read:

*Here sitted Paddy*
*The king at Lennon's Cross*
*They that mocked this town*
*History proved they lost.*

Padrig Moore

*Oh, the violence began near our home, Michael,*
*When the strangers they came o'er the say*
*But this is the only ould town, son*
Where they got neither whiskey or tay.

# The Warrior

That's how it was with Paddy: when it hit him, it just flowed. What I was begging to realize was what my dad had often attempted to teach me. There was a certain peace in being with Paddy. I had failed miserably to generate enough belief in my dad's teaching to understand that he was correct when he suggested that "Faith works in strange ways".

In a curious way, I was beginning to discover that there was no need to ask questions in Crossmaglen; answers would come in their own good time. But therein lay a host of what seemed to me to be even more acutely complex equations. I was employing a lot of lead back then at the Barrack Corner, but there again, there was that mischievous glint in Paddy's left eye which incidentally had the habit of sometimes appearing in his right eye, and if I was forced to admit it, there were times when I couldn't follow it or pin it down because there was so much activity going on around the surface of Paddy's face – and I'd rather do time sooner than perjure myself or worse still, be labelled as an uneducated eejit by Paddy.

The eventual truth of the whole matter might be closer if I were to assist readers in being sympathetic to my prevailing conditions in Crossmaglen at that period in time. Suffice it to say, in the most positive vein I can announce, there is no other place in this wide, earthly world like Crossmaglen, absolutely none, not even remotely, really, and readers who are preparing to go there, be warned: your understanding of the English tongue will be of no great benefit to you.

Now, don't get me wrong; Crossmaglen folk do have a perfect grasp of the English language but their skilful restructuring of what is to them an inferior foreign language imposed on a Celtic race is so employed as to leave the rest of the English-speaking folks out in the cold. What the strangers are hearing is not what the inner message is all about; "it's Celtic riddle talk".

I learned very quickly and painfully that what the strangers are allowed to hear – or more to the point, what they think they are hearing or have heard – is not what is being exchanged, not even remotely akin to the inner message whatsoever. I feel it's important to approach this subject from many varying perspectives because of its complexity, but to fully analyse it or become an authority or expert in it, forget it.

Paddy reached into the left pocket of his "inside coat", as he described the tweed jacket beneath his gabardine raincoat. He retrieved two teaspoons which he instantly had alternating around each side of his middle finger on his left hand. The tea-stained silver blended in with the nicotine stains on Paddy's left thumb and index finger in a fashion similar to a young fox among heather on an Irish bog bank.

There was music flowing out from the open window of the cab of the Ford 7000 tractor which was parked to our left.

"It's bad ould brukily weather, Paddy," the driver commented as he dismounted outside the chemist shop next door to the Barrack Corner.

"No matter, Brian. Tomorrow will be much better," Paddy responded as he played the spoons on his left thigh.

Tommy Makem of the famous Makem and Clancy Brothers' group was educating us from within the tractor cab regarding his youthful exploits relating to rambling and gambling and being a long way from home.

"If they were all as straight about spaking up for South Armagh as Makem is," Paddy said, "more people around the world would know about our plight here in Cross."

Paddy said,

> *"Let us have faith that right makes might and in that faith let us till the end dare to do our duty as we understand it."*

"Bad scrant to Makem and the moonshine, gasson, he bruck me ould line of thought. Where was I anyway?"

"Bad ould bruckly weather, Paddy."

It was the Ford tractor driver, speaking again on his way from the chemist shop.

"Ah trought abin mesowel,(indeed upon my soul) Brian, if it rains between them showers it will be a wet day, avick. I see you have Makem with you, Brian, more power to you. Take him easy through the guttery gaps and make sure you count the creamery cans," Paddy said as Brian pulled out of town. "Where were we, gasson?"

I had no idea where Paddy was or where he was leading me. I was trying to get some sort of handle or mastery over this Crossmaglen communication technique, difficult as it was proving, or as Paddy termed it, "the Crosseology of Creative Celtic Circular Cultural Codology and Crucifixion or the Seven C's, gasson."

Then he was off again with another quick verse:

> *"What'll we do*
> *When the kittle boils over?*
> *Biddy, turn round*
> *There's a man in the bed."*

Paddy was playing the tin whistle now. Just then a couple entered the Square from the Inniskeen direction of County Monaghan.

"Just up the road there, gasson, is Paddy Kavanagh's country."

I noticed the couple were travelling side car style in a caravan, it was time for the ould craic again.

#

Margaret Barry 1960.

# Margaret Barry in Crossmaglen

The woman who was playing a banjo, was Margaret Barry, the famous Irish street ballad singer. Her man –her man in Cross for the day, at any rate, the man who had been driving the pony in the caravan – stopped and tied the pony to the cattle mart rails. Paddy kept on playing, you know how it goes – *From glen to glen, and down the mountain side, 'tis I'll be there in sunshine or in shadow* – and the banjo-plucking lady crossed the square west, which eventually leads to Castleblaney. She was a fiery-looking damsel.

"Always look for the brown label porter bottle," Paddy told me, "if they're carrying it about them, chances are it will be Castrol oil for the throat or grace before verse."

The piebald handler joined his banjo-plucking companion five yards north-west of where Paddy was pushing out 'Danny Boy' from his tin whistle. The damsel began strumming, her man friend applied some rosin to the bow of his fiddle, Paddy retired his tin whistle to his hip pocket, and he began to sing.

> "*Ooooh-ho Danny boy*
> *Oh Danny, Danny ye boy ye*
> *There's clay pipes at the Barrack Corner calling*
> *'Tis you must come*
> *Cause I think their empire's faw–awh–linn*
> *Just go to Crosse—ma—glen*
> *And look for Paddy*
> *And see the strangers*
> *Walking backway as they go*
> *'Tis there you'll find out*
> *All about your background*
> *And you'll find out things*
> *You must not know.*

Paddy lit another Woodbine cigarette. The smoked curled up in 2-inch diameter rings above his head.

"One, two, three, four rings, eight inches apart, four provinces in a 32-county island, gasson."Then he went on with more quotes.

*"When nature removes a great man, people explore the horizon for a successor, but none comes, and none will. His class is extinguished with him. In some other and quite different field the next man appears."* (Ralph Waldo Emerson)

"Emerson wasn't that slow," Paddy said. "But getting back to me ould craic about Patrick's letter, the schoolmaster was still taking laves out of my cap. He read them out as follows:

*And for this reason I long had a mind to write but hesitated till now. I was afeared of exposing myself to the talk of men because I have not studied like the others, who thoroughly imbibed law and sacred scripture, and never had to form the language of their childhood days but were able to make it still more perfect.*

"In our case what I had to say had to be translated into a tongue foreign to me as can be easily proved from the savour of my writing. It betrays how little instruction and training I have had in the art of words.."

Paddy's eyes were dancing within their sockets as he continued his craic. "The scripture says, gasson, that by the tongue will be discovered the wise man and understanding and knowledge and the teaching of truth."

The master read on, Paddy explained, as follows:

*But what helped is an excuse, however true, especially if combined with presumption since now in me old age I strive for something that I did not acquire in my youth. It was my sins that prevented me from fixing in my mind what before I could barely read through, but who believes me.*

"'Though I should repeat what I started out as a youth, nay almost as a boy not able to speak I was taken captive before I knew what to pursue or what to avoid. Hence today I blush with fear to reveal my lack of education for I' am unable to tell my story to those versed in the art of concise writing, in such a way, I mane to say, as my spirit and my mind long to do and so that the sense of words expresses what I feel. God bless Crossmaglen"

The master read on "out of the contents of me ould cap, gasson," Paddy continued, "and he said,

*"It was given unto me, it was given unto others then I should not be silent in my desire of thanksgiving, and if some folk think me arrogant for doing so in spite of my lack of knowledge and my slow tongue, it is after all written, the stammering tongues shall quickly learn to spake peace."*

Paddy was whistling again, then he began humming what sounded like one of those familiar church hymns.

*Were you there?*
*When the strangers*
*Sacked our town*
*Were you there on the Square?*
*Did you see them in the air?*
*Were you there when the strangers*
*Sacked our town?*
*Were you there where the mart was on the Square?*
*When our town hall held our emblem o'er us fair*
*Did you hear the sound of pigs?*
*Did you know they killed off gigs?*
*Were you there when we circled round in prayer?*
*Did you sit at bridge of Creggan?*
*Where the "Red Hand" points to Heaven*
*Were you there?*
*Did you spake with Druid men, did you stroll*
*McCooey's glen – were you there?*
*Were you there in the Barony of the Fews?*
*Did you sit on our ring forts?*
*Drink their hush in morning dews?*
*Were you there when the strangers sacked our town?*
*Did you smell the fragrance of sloe bush?*
*Were you there?*
*Did you walk the Pigs Dyke?*
*Did you ceilidh every night?*
*Were you there?*
*When the strangers*
*Sacked our town.*

Pat McEntegart

Paddy was present, he said, "behind the ditch on top of the Mill Hill in Monog one morn next to the graveyard wall. It was a very still Autumn morn, leaves were falling, the wind was a soft one from the west. It carried the prayer of an old woman, bare-kneed on the granite slab in front of the Celtic cross just north of the Creggan dure."

Somebody told Paddy that it was the grave of Barney Morris, a young Republican shot dead by Freestaters in the 1920's.

"The ould woman must have been hard of hearing cause she prayed out very loud, she prayed as follows:

> *"If I should live to be a right ould age*
> *May I always howl on to me bit of individuality*
> *Pon me sowel and me charm and wit*
> *That I may not be discarded when I am withered*
> *Worn and weak*
> *But sought after and cherished*
> *Like a fine ould antique."'*

That same evening after mass in Saint Patrick's church on the Newry road, Crossmaglen, it was time to visit the graveyard. We proceeded out the door on the north side of the church, or "the Creggan dure", as Paddy described it as he dove his left hand into the holy water font by the side of the church wall.

The amount of oxygen which abounds around you; nowhere else in this universe can its comparison be found. I became preoccupied with my pocket handkerchief. Paddy was now praying out loud in muffled tones, holding his cap over the lower part of his body in fig-leaf fashion. I leaned my ear forward, careful to avoid detection, in between shoulder jerks and foot shuffling in the granite chips on the grave surface.

"I pray that those who believe and fear God," he was saying, "whosoever designs to look at or receive writing which my learned friend is placing upon paper, which has been composed by Patrick, a sinner much unlearned, in Crossmaglen, that nobody should ever say that it was me ignorance if I did or showed forth anything, however small, according to God's good pleasure, but let this be their conclusion before I die."

He wiped the moss and marble chippings off the knees of his corduroy trousers, then made the sign of the cross and lit a Woodbine cigarette. The east wind drew swift Celtic circles above us in the sharp winter's sky.

# The Cross of Lennon

*Burning Ulster buses – ease of pain*
*Uplifted paving slabs – anger – disrepair*
*In the distance, 'squeal' of strangers' pigs [army Saracen cars]*
*Drunk on high octane*
*Street incandescents blinded to the 'Square'*
*Frightened Christians – pushed too far for prayer*
*'Jack's Hut' no more – two Mary Kates are gone*
*Strange accents – polished faces – raids at dawn*
*Civil – yes – disobedience was taught and wrought*
*Bernadette and Rory Mac, one vote they sought*
*Teachers of Gaelic locked in a dungeon without breach*
*Prepare again – Mass rock to preach*
*The sergeants' car upended in their lawn*
*The blue crown lantern no more above their door*
*A trinity of batterers facing south*
*Theme of battering ram – to even score*

Pat McEntegart

I wondered about the lone headstone of blue slate standing erect between the church door and the water font where Paddy made the sign of the cross on his chest with his left hand. The lone headstone had a triplicate of curved arches somewhat similar to the Alamo.

"Remember the Alamo, gasson? There were a lot of good Irishmen lost their lives in the Alamo, and there's them bloody eejits" – he nodded in the direction of the British soldiers – "up there in the big house on the Culloville road, gasson, and they are painting banners with red paint saying, 'Remember the Alamo'.

"Well, they had better remember that Davey Crocket was an Irishman and all his good men were Irish, too, who lost their lives in the Alamo, so there's no need to rub salt in the wound. There will come a day when they will be making banners saying 'Remember Crossmaglen'."

I read the partially visible inscription: *Herein a gentle mother lies.* The stone bore the name Gaffney.

"That family lived on top of Monog Hill. They got it hard, gasson. The landlord, Ball, was bad to them. Many's the hard struggle they had before the landlord came with the battering ram and knocked down their chimney and cabin. That poor crater of a woman died alongside the broad road."

"But it's a long road and there's no turn off" Paddy turned towards the parochial house. I had the feeling that his eyes were watering up somewhat. He walked north approximately ten yards through the burial grounds, then knelt down at a tall Celtic cross which bore the inscription *Morris* erected by his comrades and made the sign of the cross on his chest. The frosty sunlight smarted my eyes; they stung slightly.

Perhaps my eyes had been watering all the time. Crossmaglen touches you deeply; it triggers your senses. The air is so pure, there are high amounts of oxygen which abound around you. Nowhere else in this universe can its comparison be found.

Now I was caught between green horning and long horning – I was sworn to secrecy and forbidden to ask questions.

"Well you were looking for work, gasson, and far be it from me to deprive you. Did I tell you about the eleven days the Brits lost back in 1752?"

"The whole country stood stopped in their tracks from September 3rd till the 15th that year. Do you think maybe that's why they are so far behind us here in Cross, gasson? Maybe that's why they made those cruel laws against the local Irish fishermen in 1777; sure, it wasn't right nor lucky to force the Irish fishermen to smear their nets with tar and oil which chased the fish away while the English fishermen were allowed to preserve their nets with the bark from oak trees! The world should be towel about this, pon me sowel. It wasn't our fault that they were operating on the wrong calendar, and I'll tell you, gasson, if the English were to meet another Gregorian or Julian to stop them in their tracks for another eleven days, eleven hours might be enough for the boys around this town to get the upper hand on them.

"The way I see things going, gasson, there's a Crossmaglen question and there's another one wrote all over your face, avick, and your question started the minute you stepped out of that taxi cab at the Barrack Corner. You're wondering, who do we think we are? Pon me sowel, and it's a great question, but I can only spake for meself, and you know something? You might be able to figure that one out, pon me sowel. Well the Bejazz-us, avick, I be listening to all these craics about strong white men training great chiefs how to stand on top of high rocks in strange places and put their hands to their mouths and make loud noises to attract their neighbours.

"These boyos also be telling Paddy craics about warriors with twigs in both hands touching them together to get smoke signals sent to a bunch of fellas on another faraway hill or outpost. It bates me, gasson, if there's any truth coming out of Shorts Snug atall, atall, with all that's going on between us and the Bejas." The Bejas are an African tribe. "At the present time we don't know who we are, but I'll just tell you, we know who we're not.

"Tell me this, avick, just when am at it: What do you make of this, gasson?"

Paddy showed me the "strokes of the quill", as he described the small sketch he removed from beneath the left leg of his thermal underwear ("me drawers, gasson—these are me drawers").

I was expecting to hear my Dad's voice; in fact, I was praying for it to penetrate the airways of my thick skull at that moment. I surveyed what appeared to me to be samples of what

were Hindu drawings that Paddy handed to me. What could I make of it?

Here I was in Crossmaglen, listening to stories of the White Man teaching Cherokee chiefs. Earlier I had handed my boarding pass to an Oriental flight attendant who greeted me with "aOlluh". I was hearing about men on Cappy Rock sending "Ah Hoooooy there" signals to Lissaraw Street, I was reviewing Hindus with their Hu-Hu, I was seeing strangers from another country walking backways spelling the Greek alphabet out loud as they went – alpha, india, bravo, alpha, amigo – or perhaps they were praying out loud to quench their fears.

I couldn't at this early stage establish with any degree of certainty if it was the biblical quote.

*I am the alpha and the Omega that was emanating from the red lips centred in the sea of polish on the stranger's face behind the windshield of what appeared to me as a miner's hardhat with a bush growing out of it.*

"What do you make of it all?"

Give me a break here, Paddy, I thought. I need the work – but maybe it's time to speak to my shop Steward Just then Dad tuned in.

"Halleluiah – you know what they did to the Wright Brothers, son, when they declared they had invented a machine that could fly?" Dad said. "Remember what I told you was contained in the note young Edison was sent home with by his teacher to his mum?"

Dad had told me that Edison's lifespan at school lasted a mere three months. His teacher sent him home carrying her opinion on paper. Edison's teacher decided that his mum should be advised her son could not be taught. Luckily for the world, Mrs Edison had enough wisdom to examine both sides of the paper. On the blank side Mrs Edison informed the teacher that the word "educate" was derived from the Latin words *en dues* (to draw from within).

Paddy was eyeing me hard as he filled his Peterson pipe with Carrols No. 1 tobacco he had teased out from his pouch. I wondered if perhaps he might be admiring my progress with the Cross green-horning thesis. Not a word was spoken between us at this juncture in my thought pattern. If, as Dad had suggested, education comes from within, then surely the question I must ask myself was, how could I employ Mrs Edison's motivational skills in the presence of Paddy? The striking of the Swan match against the Barrack Corner stone, coupled with Paddy's request to borrow my "manly torso for a wind breaker, gasson", momentarily interrupted my thoughts.

"A lighter job would suit you, gasson," he said in between puffs of smoke and red-hot ashes emanating from his left index finger. The punctured Guinness bottle top was then re-placed over the ignited leaves. "Stick to the lead, gasson. Drawing education out of me, gasson? Well, I'll tell ye: I don't think you would be able to stay around Cross long enough for that one."

# The Disruption

*Come gather around, boys*
*And I'll tell you a story*
*It's all about Ireland*
*And these troubled times*

*I'll tell you how England*
*Is treating the north, boys*
*By having her soldiers*
*Keep our men tied down*

*They arrested our young men*
*And put them in prison*
*Because they loved Ireland*
*And worked for her cause*

*But all that this country*
*Wish for to see, boys*
*Is Ireland free*
*From those ould English laws.*

(Composer unknown to author)

Reader, I need your help here. Where was I? Paddy had read my mind accurately again, but I remembered that Edison was unsuccessful 9999 times before he invented the light bulb. God grant me strength in Crossmaglen, I prayed as I gazed across the pens of the cattle mart towards the spire of Saint Patrick's church. What was this magnetic pull I was feeling?

Here I was, 365 feet above sea level, Ireland's version of the windows of the world. My feeling right then was one of elated excitement. Could I possibly bottle this unique energy, sponge-like, enthusiastic rebounding spirit generated by such a beleaguered Christian community.

I watched as the strangers disrupted a handball game being played by the Billiard Room Corner by local youths. This is a high gable wall on the western side of Cross Square, at the opening of an alley which leads to North Street. The youths were being forced at gunpoint to face the alley wall, and the phrase, 'for unlawful knowledge', was being floated across the Square by the strangers.

There was a strange mix of international or bi-continental words floating around the bush-growing, hardhat ensemble. Here I must explain some European abbreviations employed by the strangers in the beginning of the seventh decade of the 1900's lest there be any confusion. In New York, for example, the 'FIB' might correctly be construed to be short for the Federal Investment Bank, but in Crossmaglen, Paddy explained, "'FIB' has been adopted to refer to our present generation of 'High-Tech Computer Scientists' as 'Fenian Irish Bastards'."

"Okay, okay – sticks and stones etc., and what we don't know won't sicken us etc., etc. But tell me this, gasson, and yer seeing this for the first time: do you see them gassons with their wee bits of personal belongings spread out over the street and the strangers reading through them? Would you stand idly by, gasson, on any street in the world and see your kit and kin pistol-whipped and victimized by strangers from another country? If the strangers find your wallet while they are searching you and they find something within it by reading your personal letters and papers, they then can use it against you, or worse still, use it against you as emotional blackmail. Do you get me point, gasson?"

I watched as the local youths were forced at gunpoint to stand in spread-eagled fashion, their legs four feet apart at the ankles, their toes four feet away from the base of the alley wall. Their arms were outstretched above their shoulders; their bodies were prevented from moving forward towards the wall only by the tips of the index finger of each hand, hands turning crystal white in the freezing, penetrating east wind mixed with sleet and rain.

I watched dumbfounded as the strangers forcibly frisked the helpless youths of tender years amid tears and laughter. The Crossmaglen youths "had something not visible to the naked eye, removed from them by the strangers at the Billiard Room corner that January evening in 1971," Paddy said later, and I agreed with him. It was an undignified gesture by the strangers, armed with rifles, to grope the genitals of the youths in full public view of the passers-by.

"For Unlawful Cross Knowledge " [fuck] the strangers," Paddy said with tears in his eyes. "Did you ever study how diamonds are made, gasson"?

"Can't say I've paid much attention to it, Paddy."

"They are formed under severe pressure, usually between very hard rocks, avick. There's no scarcity of hard rock round Cross. Do you think we'll cut a few diamonds in the rough round South Armagh, gasson?"

Then he was off on another of his roller-coaster quoting trips again. At times like this Paddy's eyes would become glazed and very sad.

"I pray God grant me the wisdom and endurance to do me duty as it should be done. I must be patriotic, not partisan in practical matters. The end is not merely speculative knowledge of what is to be done, but rather the doing of it!"

Paddy cursed and prayed as the strangers assaulted one of the youths.

"Jesus Christ, gasson, did ye see that British bastard strike the kid in the face with his fist?" "Corporal Bell me arse, gasson, what do you expect from a pig only a grunt. You'll tell the world what you seen here today, gasson."

I was hoping my small camera had caught the illegal assault on the youth. The world needed to see what I had seen here today.

"It's not enough to know about virtue, gasson. My contention is this, gasson: As with virtue, so with self-control of your own destiny. We must endeavour to possess it and use it, gasson.

"As long as somebody else has charge of us, gasson, we can lay our mistakes at their dure. In our daily lives we may lack certain material comforts regarded by some as necessary by the standards of the modern world, cause the majority of our wealth is still locked up in an imperial land system, do you see? But we still have the gift of laughter and joy, a great love of music, a lack of malice and an absence of the desire for vengeance – although, we are been pushed very hard at the minute."

# Crossmaglen's Yancy

"Just look over there at what's going on at the present time at the Billiard Room corner as I spake, gasson, in our present world of injustice, revenge, fear and want. The less intelligent the stranger is, the more stupid he thinks the Cross people are. Where was I, gasson? Oh, ah, Corporal Bell, the boy bater – or 'Yancy', as he is better known around South Armagh.

"Yancy was the president of Liberia in the Thirties, the second most powerful person in that country then, gasson. Yancy operated a practise of pawning off human beings for forced labour. Me scholarly friends in Shorts Snug towel me they had a copy of a report from the US government printing office from 1931.

"There was a man's testimony in it who stated that Yancy said to him, 'If a want to ship you to Fernando Po now, I can do so, who can stop me? I can turn you over to the soldiers to take you to the barracks in the interior and then give them orders to kill you on the way, and when the report gets back to Monrovia I will simply write the president and tell him you died on the way from sickness, and whatever reason I give for your death will be accepted by him.'

"Now when I was a gasson meself round these parts, the schoolmaster Magee and Miss Grant always handed us a bundle of magazines every month by the name of *The Far East*. Kate the Tinker read a story in one of them magazines for me one day and I never forgot it. Kate towel me there was a tribe of people somewhere in Africa that suffered the most under this Yancy boyo."

"Kate the Tinker said their names were Wadebo. I remember hearing the ould song their children used to sing, gasson. Maybe it's time the people of Cross learned it, judging by the way things are going on here with the present Yancy."

# Yancy

*We were there when trouble came to our people*
*For this reason, Yancy came to our country*
*He caught our husbands and our brothers*
*Sailed them to Nan-Po*
*And there they die*
*And there they die*
*Tell us, Yancy, why?*
*Yancy, why?*

*Wadebo women have no husbands*
*Yancy, why?*
*Wadebo women have no brothers*
*Tell us*
*Yancy, why?*

*Mothers, fathers, sons and daughters died*
*Waiting for their return*
*Yancy, why?*
*Why?*

"According to me scholarly trio," Paddy continued, our Yancy or Corporal Bell or whatever other name he goes under – the stranger who was baten the youth at the Billiard Room corner, he had the gall to brag about it to some of them American writers, gasson.

"Those schoolmasters of mine, no matter what they say about them or the wee sup of the crater[whiskey], all them things aside, and bearing in mind that Robby Burns was at his very best whenever he had a jug of punch by him," Paddy said, "for the sake of health we'll take a sup etc. Do you know what they towel me, gasson? They said yer man Corporal Bell, the modern Yancy, this Corporal Bell towel an American reporter that he could do what he liked with the gassons who lived in South Armagh. He said he had a free hand, and worse than that, this modern Yancy was expecting a medal for throwing Irish youths in among pigs. (army Saracens)

"This fella, Bell, kicking and slapping and thumping South Armagh youths inside of 'pigs'!(saraceens) I mane to say the masters towel me there was a picture of this fella Bell in *Life Magazine*. There was four pages of him bragging about his famous British brutality, and here's us looking at him in broad daylight in front of our own two eyes. Have ye plenty of lead in that pencil of yours, gasson?"

"It's a long road, there's no turn on, and even Shorts Lane and the Mill Lane have turns on them," Paddy said sadly. Then he brightened. "I never finished me ould craic about Mulligan's Cais. Come to think about it, there's several craics I didn't finish, and the chances are there will be several more. Of course, that depends on how much work you can take in round Cross, gasson."

Just then I noticed that the youths who had earlier been playing handball by the Billiard Room corner wall were being frogmarched past us in single file en route to the British army base on the Culloville road, escorted by heavily armed soldiers with menacing faces.

"Keep yer trousers on no matter what!" Paddy said to the youths as they passed by. Just then a heavy mist began to descend all over Crossmaglen Square, and Paddy slipped into one of his melodramatic moods again.

*"De mist aside*
*And the wind the tide arose*
*And the pale king glanced at Cross*
*The field of battle*
*But no man was moving there*
*Nor a cry of Christian heard there on*
*Nor yet of heathen*
*Only the one wave*

*Brake in among dead faces*
*To and fro*
*Swaying the helpless hands*
*Up and down*

*Tumbling the hollow helmet*
*And the falling flea*
*The voice of days of ould*
*And days to be*

"Is it work you are looking for, gasson, in Crossmaglen?"

Paddy blessed himself twice, shaking his head at the same time, and then scratched his head with both hands.

"Well, it's like this, avick. Sarah was without child for almost ninety years, so who am I in God's name to question your beliefs, gasson," he said as he played tug-o-war with the peak of his cap. "I mane to say, gasson, is there a famine over in New York, or maybe you're hiding from some hot-blooded female – but that's another craic, gasson.

"I knew yer grandfather's people; yer welcome to Cross. Round these parts it's seek and you shall be fined, and it's more a case of being broke down round you while you're sleeping than knock and it shall be opened unto you.

"There has been plenty of tearing asunder going on here, too. Look down there at the market house clock – look what them strangers did to it. Have you any of that fudgy colour thingamajig" – by which he meant my camera – "with you? Don't let them see you taking pictures, gasson, or it's local doctors will be finding the work instead of you.

Paddy extended to me his right hand; I met his halfway with my own minus the pencil, while we were still entwined in a firm, characteristic handshake, Paddy began to sing:

> "*Crossmaglen, I love you*
> *You're the pillow of my dreams*
> *Your soil I'll wear beneath my nails*
> *I'll wash them in your streams*
>
> *Pick up your shovel, Crossmaglen*
> *And in hand a flint stone too*
> *Scrape your soil unto your land*
> *It belongs to me and you*
> *Don't fret about that foreign band*
> *Watch them dig their mould so blue*
> *Crossmaglen, I love you*
> *You are Celtic through and through*

*Crossmaglen, this be my task*
*If task it be not pain*
*To cause mankind upon this earth*
*Admit they heard and came*

*For they shall know that my soul*
*Is to your soul juxtaposed*
*For we held what bled*
*Your thorny stem*
*Then as yet we'll smell your rose".*

Pat McEntegart

# Personal Courage

Paddy said that "John F. Kennedy towel me a craic one night sitting at the fire in Cross. I was drinking a mug of tay, gasson, and buttering a heel of a McNamee's loaf. Kennedy passed no remarks about what I was up to at all but I was listening just the same to what the bold senator was telling me, gasson. I never forgot it, either.

"Kennedy towel me to go not where the path leads but go instead where there was no path and leave a trail for others to follow. Kennedy spent a long time in hospital in the month of October 1954 with back trouble. Doesn't it bate the divil the way the ould arthritis plagues the Irish? I have the same problem meself, gasson."

"Bad back or no bad back, Kennedy didn't let the grass grow under his feet while he was out of action. What did the bold senator do but write a book, and what was the name of that book but *Personal Courage*. N'awful pity I can't read, gasson," Paddy sighed, then he slipped into one of his oratory poses.

I was mildly pleased with my progress in my green-horning studies. Having monitored Paddy's mannerisms on a couple of previous occasions, I now knew that each time he felt a Celtic rumbling coming upon him,

Paddy religiously would catch hold of the left shoulder strap of his navy blue dungarees, and with his left thumb at the rear of the bib fastener where the silver metal breast button held the strap to the body, he would make a forward thrust with the full strength of his left arm upon the dungaree strap until his arm was at 90 degrees to his chest.

In the split second before he released his hold, it was possible for me to establish the colour of Paddy's Sunday trousers, which were otherwise concealed beneath his dungarees. When Paddy pulled hard enough on his shoulder strap, his action had the effect of lifting his overall leg approximately six inches on one side of his body. As the underpants were waist-length, they remained at their original elevation, and that was my cue for a story.

"Didn't it bate the divil, gasson, that Gladstone" – the four-time Liberal Prime Minister of Great Britain and campaigner for home rule for Ireland – "only visited Ireland once?" he said. "Gladstone only stayed three weeks. N'awful pity he never made it to Cross, gasson, n'awful shame altogether. Shure them boyos couldn't understand us at all."

> *Great glorious and free,*
> *Bright flower of the earth*
> *And first gem of the sea Ireland.*

"Then there was your man Lord Palmerston talking about us in the House of Commons in England in 1860. Pon me sowel, gasson, you should have heard him," Paddy exclaimed, then began to recite the words of the British cabinet minister:

> "*Now, sir, great complaints have been made and in many respects justly about the tide of emigration which was set out from Ireland towards the shores of America, but how that any change in the relations of landlord and tenant is to check that emigration has not to my mind been satisfactorily explained by anybody who has taken part in this debate. It has been well observed that no great agricultural improvements can be made except upon large holdings and with large capital.*

*"Everybody knows that the great majority of the tenants of Ireland have but small holding of some five, ten or fifteen acres, nor have they the capital to improve any large quantity of land which they might hold, but what does that condition of Ireland arise from? Is it not from the mis-government of England?*

*"'England has nothing to do with the sub-division of holdings by which an immense and a lot of people have thought a redundant population has been created in Ireland. It arose from the very cause which is now held out as the remedy of the evils complained of; it arose from comparative fixity of tenure.'*

"What do you make of it, gasson? The years 1798, 1848, 1867, 1915 and 1969 were linked together in Paudrig Pearse's words:

*"'We of the Irish Volunteers and ye others who are associated with us, know only one definition of freedom: it is Tone's definition, it is Mitchell's definition, it is Rossa's definition. They think they have foreseen everything, but the fools, the fools, the fools! They have left us our Fenian dead, and while Ireland holds these graves, Ireland unfree shall never be at peace.'"*

# The Cappy Duel
## (which was illegal and most unusual)

One night when he was a slip of a lad Paddy was sitting behind the settle bed beside "the upper room dure" He was supposed to be in bed, but "the craic was that good, there's divil the sleep would come over me."

Johnny the Diddle was telling a craic about two brothers who were going to set a duel the next week in the half acre in front of Kate the Tinker's cottage, and as Paddy said, "How in hell's blazes could you be expected to go to sleep with a craic like that starting?"

He said it was worth every swipe of the wet dishcloth he got across the back of his neck to stay upto hear thre story. The brother's names were Peadar and Eoin, and the reason they were holding the duel was because they couldn't agree on how to divide a field they were after inheriting.

74

"Pon me sowel, gasson, I had to cross me legs real tight to keep from wetting the clay flure behind the settle bed. That was a big problem, as if we hadn't enough problems in Cross, but if you were unfortunate enough to become short-taken at the exciting part of the craic you weren't supposed to be listening to in the first place, well, pon me sowel, gasson, the bloody stain would stay in the clay flure for days. And even if you got up in a hurry and crept away unnoticed, bad scrant to the clay but it would stick between your legs and get mixed up with the straw from the settle bed and the chaff from the busted tick. And if the cowl, wet dish-cloth wasn't rough enough on your tender ears and neck, pon me sowel, gasson, can you imagine what effect a mixture of hot steaming water, limestone and bog mould would have on parts of your body that were never exposed to the elements?

"According to Johnny the Diddle, Peader couldn't sleep for several nights before the duel, and the bit of sleep Eoin was getting was constantly being interrupted by a room full of fairies dancing about and spreading sheaves of ferns from Lissaraw Fort all over the bed.

"Johnny said that the king of the fairies towel Eoin that he could choose between three companions who would accompany him to the duel. Johnny said the Fairy King had approached Peadar with the same offer, but Peadar had a woeful headache from the night before and he made a swipe at the Fairy King with the back of his hand."

"Johnny said Peadar was as thick as a double ditch and when he made the swipe at the Fairy King across the two bonacks of bread that was standing up against the staff churn behind the goat's stall, alongside the fan-bellows, he missed the Fairy King and caught the hurricane lamp in between the bonnacks of bread, broke the globe in the lamp and sent one of the bonnacks of bread into the churn full of buttermilk. The staff of the churn fell and hit the goat that was sleeping under the churn, the goat bolted and broke the rope that was tying her to the leg of the churn. The Fairy King picked up the hurricane lamp and hung it on the goat's horns, climbed up on the goat's back, went twice around the kitchen, mounted the settle bed, and as the half-dure was open (cause how else would the Fairy King have gotten in?), the King and goat jumped the half-dure and vowed never to return regardless of which brother won the duel."

Paddy chuckled. "Wasn't it dacent of the Fairy King to rescue the goat from such a dysfunctional gathering?"

There was a small snag in the offer the Fairy King had made to Eoin, however. He was to pick one of the three companions himself.

Paddy said Johnny the Diddle was a big, long, lanky kind of a man, who had to get down on his hunkers to keep from hitting his head on the horse's collar which rested above the fireplace as he attempted to light a wee stub of a clay pipe he held in his mouth with his lips, and he remembered clearly that Johnny had no teeth.

"You could hear a pin dropping in the next townland," Paddy continued, "as they waited for Johnny to light his pipe. That was before the clothesline broke and fell in the ashes and frightened the clucking hen out of her nest on top of the turf stack.

The first companion appeared to Eoin. The Fairy King told Eoin that this fellow went by the name of Fear.

"Eoin knew full well that the best he could hope for with Fear was to run away, but then he would always be known as a coward."

The Fairy King then introduced the second fellow as Strength. This fellow sounded a bit more promising, but Eoin was warned again by the Fairy King that Strength had his weak points . Eoin would still be vulnerable to injury or death.

Johnny the Diddle was quick to point out that Eoin was facing death anyway, no matter which way he turned. The fairy king then told Eoin that he had one more choice, and this fellow went by the name of Love.

"You should have heard Johnny going on about the qualities of this fellow Love. Then Johnny said the Fairy King towel Eoin that Love possessed all the qualities of Fear and Strength put together, and there was nothing unseemly about him."

By this time Paddy was busting to get to the chamber pot below the bed in the upper room, but there was a three-legged, five-week-old piglet stretched out straight across his path to the door with a porter bottle full of milk stuck in the side of his mouth.

"The pig's mother was suckling 14 of its brothers and sisters and she had only 12 teats," Paddy explained. A couple of delicate ones were obliged to take turns at the turf fire besides Paddy's younger brother who no longer took his bottle to bed; he seemed to be getting more substance from his thumb. That was the reason why the dummy tit was placed on the porter bottle for the delicate piglet/

"And anyhow I would have missed the best part of Johnny's craic if I'd gone, so I just kept crossing me legs and squeezing them together. There was water coming out of me eyes", but it could have been worse, pon me sowel."

Johnny said that the duel was arranged to take place on the top of Cappy Rock one mile south of Cross at noon on the 17th of May, the day of the big fair in Dundalk when all the farmers would be away selling their worn-out plough horses, because all the crops were in.

Paddy's mother and father had by now forgotten about Paddy behind the settle bed. Johnny told everyone around the turf fire that night about Peadar and Eoin being a bit odd and how the brothers didn't want anyone to see them making eejits of themselves on top of Cappy Rock in the middle of broad daylight.

"Johnny the Diddle said when it came to the morn of the 17th, Peadar was using the only three-legged stool the brothers had to milk the goat. Did I tell you that the brothers lived in the same house, gasson?

"Eoin got as far as the low meadow to milk his miley goat which was shackled to Peadar's longhorn with the left blind tit. Eoin milked with his left hand while he kept a howlt of the horny goat with his right hand. Johnny said Peadar was looking up at the other field facing Albert Werley's spring well, wondering who would be building the March ditch, and Peadar was wondering to himself who would be sitting on the milking stool the next morning."

Johnny said that as big a pair of eejits as the brothers were, at least they were weighing up the consequences of their actions. Johnny said the proposed duel took place several centuries before there were any other duels or several surprise duels. Johnny said it was a terrible shame on society that the enemies of this country hadn't learned anything from the result of this brotherly dispute on the 17th of May in the 18th century.

Johnny said that when the pair of goats was milked and the turf cut in the bog, "there was flax to be drowned and dung to be thrust on the dunghill in the haggard and tay to be made and water to be carried from the spring well and Carrick lime to be steeped for whitewashing and barrels of water to be filled for pratie spraying down the Cool road, then there was a cow to be taken to the bull and a bizzen house to be repaired, and all this had to be done before noon cause the brother had to be cleaned and ready at their appointed place on Cappy Rock."

Johnny the Diddle said Peadar and Eoin never worked as hard before in all their lives. He said there was steam rising out of their ears, noses and eyes and them working side by side with each other and not speaking as if their lives depended on it. Johnny told all this to the people gathered round the turf fire, but Paddy heard him, too, because the clucking hen turned in her nest and let a few juk-juks out of her that wakened the piglet and his squeals roused Paddy who was just nodding off with the ticking of the grandfather clock on the wall beside the settle bed that he had been resting his head on.

Paddy said he couldn't get into the settle bed because there was a couple of orphan lambs being suckled by Johnny the Diddle's collie bitch that he kept purposely for the job. He said that must have been the reason for him making his ceilidh in the first place.

Johnny said that when Peadar and Eoin finally got all their chores done, they left the house and headed for Cappy Rock. They went down through Lissaraw Street and over the Drumbee mass pad. Johnny said Eoin cut himself shaving with the cut-throat razor, so he was the last out of the house. Eoin was praying out loud as he crossed the stone stile at Peter Mickel's, and kept looking up at Lissaraw Fort to see if there was any sign of yer man Love putting in an appearance."

He couldn't be certain of it because the clock struck eleven and he missed a bit of Johnny's craic, but he thought he heard him saying it was the Hard Ball and Danny who were appointed as referees and pistol controllers for the duel.

"The disputed field that caused all the commotion was just under Lissaraw Fort to the south a bit and halfway between Cappy Rock and the fort; great fairy country, gasson. Johnny said Peadar and Eoin could look straight down into the disputed field from their stand on Cappy Rock, which was over a bit to the west as they got ready to take their twenty paces."

It couldn't have been any more than twenty paces, otherwise the pair of eejits would have fallen off the rock and maybe shot themselves in the foot or worse still, shoot the Hard Ball or Danny and then the field would never be settled. Just then, something extraordinary happened.

"It wouldn't happen again, not in month of Sundays, but just when Peadar and Eoin were being reversed into each other's backs, just before their shoulder blades touched, outshot yer man, Love – bate the divil, I never got his first name but no matter. There he was, half-covered with whin blossoms and dandelion petals and torn and hawthorn blossoms, and what did Love do, gasson?

Paddy heard Johnny the Diddle saying it, at the fireside while the woman of the house lifted the gridle two notches on the swinging crane.

"Quick as a flash, before you could say Bob kissed Betty, Love had Eoin by the two shoulders and instead of being behind his big brother, Eoin found himself alongside of him, with his left shoulder touching Peadar's right shoulder."

There was tea being made in the cottage that night and Bridget's Anne was setting the ash around the end tea drawer, the spout of which was facing the back door. Anne deposited the reclaimed porter bottle into a saucepan of warm water containing four duck eggs. Johnny slid his spitting pontoon to one side with his strong leather boot. Johnny let his heavy left arm slide down off the armrest of the settle bed, where it came to a stop on Paddy's youthful forehead.

Paddy could still remember the warmth of Johnny's firm touch, a kind of inner connection with the craic Johnny was bringing to a close.

"Johnny said Peadar and Eoin looked at each other. They both must have felt the tingle of each other's pulse. Love towel the Fairy King that Peadar and Eoin had hate in their bodies hotter than any fire Cromwell ever lit in Ireland. Peadar was facing west and Eoin was facing east, and what did Love do next but stand in front of the two brothers and disarm them of their pistols, and into each of their hands he placed a haw-torn twig."

Johnny the Diddle stood with his cap removed from his head. Bridget's Anne was preparing hot milk for her bedside drink. Some of the men folk were already on their knees, ready to recite the rosary. Paddy said he had been on his knees all through Johnny's craic due to circumstances beyond his control.

"Johnny was facing the Sacred Heart picture when he repeated Love's words to Peadar and Eoin that 17th of May morn on Cappy Rock. Love said, 'When all fruit fails your welcome haw.'

Peadar and Eoin made a covenant in the presence of the Hard Ball and Danny with Love as a witness. They divided their field by planting a hedge and building a stone ditch, into which they planted the hawthorn twig that Love had given them. The fruits of Love's efforts can be seen to this present day just below Lissaraw Fort slightly to the west of Cappy Rock.

Peadar was facing Creevekeran in the west as he planted his hawtorn in his half of the ditch. Eoin walked further along in a northerly direction, where he had had the ould craic with the Fairy King who was on his way back up the hill to Lissaraw Fort. Love made up a trinity of persons united in giving peace a chance that day in Crossmaglen, South Armagh, as Eoin stopped midway up the previously disputed property and faced east, looking directly into Drumackavall Hills. There he planted Love's gift of compromise and reconciliation. Paddy said that Love's monument is there on the outskirts of Crossmaglen for the whole world to reflect on: When all fruit fails, your welcome haw.

# CAPPY SONGS

Mickey Joe Carraher, a Cappy man now deceased, told Paddy one time that he had a next-door neighbour named Meegan who made three-legged stools for a living. At night-time he would head off on foot to the pub in Culloville, a mile and half away. Then when he was returning home after midnight, he would always sing some lines of old songs he had known. One was *"There's only two in this wide, wide world, that's me and the man in the moon"*; another one that he sang was *"Our chimneys won't be smoking a hundred years from now"*.

> *To a Hallowed Halo Hollow*
> *This United Kingdom came*
> *To a big house beside the Cross*
> *Causing suffering and pain*
>
> *They were wearing their souls upon their face*
> *Cause I saw them myself covered in grace*
> *There was Farney-gaten and Gaelic Baten*
> *Barbed wire slashers and car light smashers*
>
> *There was tin-bean cookers and flown-in hookers*
> *Some thought they were mushrooms, others fauns*
> *When you got up in the morn they'd be all over the lawns*
>
> (Pat McEntegart)

"I'll just tell you, gasson", Paddy said as he watched the red evening sun descending behind Creevekeeran Hill, "it was reminiscent of a red ten-shilling note being slipped happily back between the warm bosom depository employed by turn-of-the-century females in the poultry market in Cross."

These women were noted for their regularity and frequency, not to mention their inexhaustible patience in waiting another day for prices to drop. Their ten-shilling notes and their pound notes were concealed in tiny silk purses within the nursing quarters of their anatomy.

"The boyos round Cross maintained the notes were sometimes heard to cry whenever these wemen were finally persuaded to wean them in exchange for a Rhode Island Red rooster or hen, as the sun settled and the cloud filled in its space symbolically, like the closed head shawl the afore-mentioned wemen used to wear in bygone days.

"A person born into the Cross stream of events has no idea; in fact, gasson, they couldn't even begin to conjure up or design a picture, or dream about the avalanche of obstacles, hurdles and ordeals to which they will most certainly be exposed to throughout their lives."

They cannot calculate how much courage they must employ to resist the temptation which will daily beset them of the sensitive shrinking from undeserved censure which they must learn to control, and the ever-recurring contest between a natural desire for public approbation and a sense of public duty. Of the load of injustice, they must be content to bear even from those that should be their friends and the imputations of their motives and the sneers and sarcasms of ignorance and malice, gasson."

Paddy said, "A Crossmaglen person will suffer all the manifold injuries which partisan or private malignity, disappointed of its objects, may shower upon their heads; auh ehh ah and forebye."

A Crossmaglen native, if they would retain their integrity, must learn to bear unmoved and walk steadily onward in the path of duty, sustained only by the reflection that time may do them justice, or if not that, after all their individual hopes and aspirations and even their name among people should be of little account to them when weighed in the balance against the welfare of a people of whose destiny they are a constituted guardian and defender.

# A Question with a Question

Reader, to be perfectly honest and candid about it, as they say around Cross, I'm unsure as to whether it was an image of Adam shaking the apple tree or if it was the minor adjustment Eve made to the fig-leaf in the picture in my mind, but the bottom line was, I was tempted and it wasn't a mild attack either. I was severely tempted in Crossmaglen and this I knew from my father's advice about acts which could be dangerous: "Don't do it son, don't even think about it," Dad said to me repeatedly. Well, did any of *you* take *your* Dad's advice when you were young?

So, I confess, I succumbed to the weakness of being human. I asked Paddy a question. Yeah, that's it, just one innocent question – I know, total sacrilege committed under the South Armagh rendition of ancient scrolls designed between ditches on the road from Carrickmacross to Crossmaglen, where I can definitely state I will never ask questions again. But you must understand I was hearing Edison's advice at that moment, to do the thing you fear and the death of fear is certain. That might work if you are sitting in a shed in New York with bad lamplight, where there wouldn't be many around to see you make an eejit of yourself. But I was standing at the Barrack Corner in Cross with armour-piercing, steel war-zone towers each side of me and in the closest of these towers, I could plainly see the infrared glow of the sentry's night-sight rifle being trained on my body. The sentry was no more than ten yards from where I stood with Paddy having our friendly discussion. That's the way it was in Crossmaglen: two worlds totally oblivious of their juxtapositions within the four sides of the largest square in Europe. Two sides within four sides; could it ever be two and two?

As I was conjuring up various headings for what I was writing, that's when my apple fell off the tree, bang on my head. It was out before I realized what had happened:

"How much is two and two, Paddy???"

Paddy looked at me, he looked away from me, he looked at the nearby mountains, he looked at the clouds, he spent some time surveying the

Mill Lane, and he looked at Carron Hill. Then it was back to me again. I was feeling dizzy, and it appeared momentarily that the Edison prophecy might be disproved at any moment in Crossmaglen.

I swallowed hard. Paddy bit into his ounce of Carroll's No. 1 tobacco across its middle with the full force of the only remaining incisor on the north east side of his atonmy. Paddy's gaze was fixed upon my rapidly whitening face. Then it began: first the shuffle of the feet, then the sudden trust of the hands in among the baler twine in both pockets, then the re-positioning of the tweed cap north-south then settled east, and finally the throat clearing in preparation for the tobacco spit. Paddy was ready for me.

"Be damn it, avick, it's a tough one. How much is two and two?" Paddy proceeded to give himself a dry shave with his left hand, then he switched hands and cupped his chin with the right hand. "Be damn, avick, you have me backed into a tight corner."

Just then I noticed the flicker. My blood pressure dropped 20 points, the green in Paddy's eyes began their swim stroke and the clay pipe began its Kerry set.

"Tell me something, gasson." He began to exude an air of Druidical aloofness. "This two and two question? Am I buying or selling?"

Paddy had me again. He had answered my question with a question. Paddy heard my confession in the dimly-lit local snug and absolution was given in the form of two Bush which "began their life in ould wooden barrels in a village in County Antrim".

"At least you had the courage to ask me the question, gasson, about the two sides of Cross square. They built a mill in Antrim for grinding down them Bush drinks and the dissolved portion was used for curing dry mourn in cows, scour in poorly fed calves, gout in bachelors, potency in fridgid wemen, and writers' cramp in ould-aged pensioners having difficulties preparing wills.

"Where was I anyway? You and your arithmetic questions," Paddy said as he broke wind with a loud burp that echoed across the square. "It's better out than the doctor."

"Talking about questions," he continued, "there's one running through me head as I spake, avick. If the shortest space between two lines is a straight line, then how does it come they drew the bloody border so crucked?"

Just then, it rained again. "Thank God for that shower," Paddy declared, "if it rains between the showers it will be a wet day, and that manes there will be all the more water flowing to the say, gasson, cause Cross is 365 feet above say level and the more rain we get in Cross the faster it will shoot past Larkin's Bridge, and the more sticks and stones it will carry with it from Culloville, Lissaraw and Mobane. By the time it goes through Coolderry bog, it will have rusty creamery cans and maybe a few gas cylinders and God knows plenty of stones.

"And if it sweeps Ellen Morgan's flure, and it runs through the Nailer's haggard, you'd never know what the tears of Cross might have mixed in them before it causes a tidal wave in the eye of the Coffin Bridge on its way to the say, and when the big waves caused by the rain in Cross hits the say, the wave will mix with others and the whole thing will head for the Wicked Sisters shore, and with a bit of luck, if we get enough rain, the waves will be strong enough to wash the soil from the Wicked Sister's" – by which he meant England's – "shore back to Ireland and we will get big and they will get small like me grandfather used to tell me."

According to Paddy, there were two sides to this craic about the rain.

"If we get no rain atall, atall, then we are still onto a winner cause the lakes will all dry up and that manes there will be more land for 5 acre farmers and the bog banks will be drier, and we can put all the bog banks back on the hills, where it was washed down from the mountains after they cut down the giant oak trees. Then the bog mould would be back on the mountains, the rugged hills would be growing more crops and the hills would be much higher, and the boys would have more places to lie out on, and they'd see strangers further away, and there would be less time spent building bungalows, and the ground I'll be harder, and the strangers won't be able to dig themselves into caves and burrows.

"And the air will be clearer, and the sounds will travel further and carry better, and the whitewash will stay on longer, and there will be no time spent cutting rushes. Straw will be cheaper, hay will be easier saved, round bales of silage will be lighter, and that manes it will take less diesel, so there will be more diesel available for colour experiments, (diesel smuggling created an extra income for the small farmers and businessmen in the area) and wee, narrow country roads will be able to carry big lorries at night. And there will be no clouds, so that manes the moon will shine every night, so the big painted X's at all the border crossings will be visible, the lorries won't need lights, everyone will know where they are going, men will be better rested, they will make more babies, there will be more help to do the milking and things, and there will be less craters appearing on lonely country roads. So either ways, gasson, Cross has a lot to look forward to whether it rains or not."

Paddy was in one of his very rare fleeting angry moments now.

"The Crucifiction at Cross. It goes like this, gasson:

*"The doings of the stations in Cross:*

*First, the agony in your own garden.*

*Second, the searching of your pillow.*

*Third, the placing of spikes and barbed wire by the crown.*

*Fourth, the pushing and dragging of you to Cross.*

*Fifth, the tying of your hands behind your back and the blaspheming of your family name.*

*Sixth, the scourging by sleep deprivation, torturous noises, and death threats.*

*Seventh, they give you something on a rusty plate that tastes like vinegar from a soap sponge.*

*Eighth, they show you 40 pieces of silver, left behind by the Judas who had to run out of town.*

*Ninth, you find strength from your adversity, just enough, you hope that secretly makes you hold on. You fight the sleep, you pray, you make a fist, you thank God for your friends, you thank God for your enemies, you pray for their blindness, their weakness. Your love of Cross overcomes all negativity.*

*Tenth, they cut you loose, throw you out on a dark country road in the middle of the night, in a hostile area. Perhaps they secretly hope Samaritans cease to travel via their Brook. You carry on, you carry your Cross."*

After this recitation Paddy started to hum another one of his 'tunes', one of those catchy Celtic foot-tappers. I soon remembered the lines from having heard it played on Sundays on *Ceol na Gael* radio programs from Fordham University in the Bronx. It had overtones of similarly styled lyrics from the deep south in America – *"hands round, turn around, pick a bale of cotton"*. Mum used to sing along to a rendition of "Hadn't we the gay old time at Phil the Flutter's ball".

But Paddy's version was one I hadn't heard before.

# Phil the Para's Fall

*Lights out, switch it off*
*Open boot and bonnet*
*Let me see your M.O.T.*
*Your windscreen's clean*
*No tax upon it*
*Hands up, call a cop*
*Turn and face the wall – (pause) – (loud bang)*
*I was standing there next to him*
*At Phil the Para's fall*
*Behind the whin*
*The light was dim the rucksack lay on top of him*
*His mates all ran away from him*
*The Wessex bird flew over him*
*At Phil the Para's fall*
*Hulda's ghost then disappeared*
*And mobile pigs then reappeared*
*When asked they said – know nothing at all*
*In Cross at Phil the Para's fall."*

# Town of Crossmaglen Proclamation

"Whereas the concerned citizens therein, and elsewhere scattered around the four winds of this earth etc., are planning to howl a public meeting on or about some weekend, or late morning, or wet day in between the showers, or some Sunday at the Creggan dure on the steps of the men's gallery if the sermon be dull, for the sole purposes of given a bit of a push to starting the ould craic around Cross again;

"And whereas this combined effort will be hereby known as 'C.R.O.S.S.', that is, the abbreviated version of the 'Cultural Rejuvenation Of Song & Story', and whereas it shall be an outstanding lifetime recreational event for families, friends and exiles, and a very much looked for event by exiles around the world and town residents and visitors with a most festive event annually for the entire family forever and ever, and when this is kick-started by meself with a bit of a trophy, it will be a source of stimulus for a bit of a hooley for thousands in the Rangers' grounds;

"And whereas people wishing to line themselves up in front of the fraternity of judges who have been appointed, themselves are to be known only by the names of Benardo, Johaton and Pauderdeen;

"All those intent on making application for the trophy should send their written requests to Box Barrack Korner, Shorts Lane, Cross, or 'B. B. K.' if you desire and, as all activities generated by this event will be tunnelled and dwelt upon in Shorts Lane by the said trinity of Benardo, Johnathon, and Pauderdeen for the sole purposes of generating work in Cross;

"Now therefore be it re-Cross'd that Paddy, the mayor and the board of trustees do here proclaim this night of January 31st 1971, town of Crosse – Cultural Rejuvenation Of Song & Story.

"Signed, Mayor Paddy X, witnessed by again and amen, no Tory republic," Paddy said.

# The Cappy Warrior

The story of the unarmed Crosse warrior, who repeatedly drove an invading battalion from Cappy Hill, kept coming to my ears through the voice of my Dad once more

The battalion was fortified on a high vantage point overlooking the outer perimeter of the ancient Dunreavy Wood next to Fetherna Bush where the three counties of Armagh, Louth and Monaghan meet. That was just a stone's throw from Mulligan's Cais beside the double bend in Coy's Lonin where Father McFadden came upon an upturned load of meadow hay one evening that was after falling off a stiff cart.

Father McFadden told Paddy the whole craic the next evening outside the confession box in the chapel which is located on the Newry road, Crossmaglen.

"He towel me he came round the corner of the lane and there was this slip of a redhead, gasson, and him with his sleeves thrusted up till his oxters. The Lord have mercy on Father McFadden (now deceased); if he was alive today he would tell you there's not a word of a lie in what am saying.

"There was the redhead forking away at the hay like there was going to be no tomorrow, Father McFadden said, and there was steam rising out of his eyes and ears. Pon me sowel, gasson, you think am codding you? Father McFadden never towel a lie in his life and him on his way to visit the sick of the parish.

"Father McFadden put his hand on the red gasson's shoulder. 'Oh boys oh boys, slow down,' he said, 'you look like you're in a bit of a panic.'

"'Begging your pardon, father, but I can't stop now. Me father would be awful mad at me.'

"'Boys oh boys, my young fella, it's not a mortal sin to stop for a drink or wipe the sweat off your brow.'

"'I can't stop now, Father, that would cause an awful racket with the ould fella.'

"'Well, I mean to say, sonny, your father sounds very tough on you. Where is he till I have a word with him? I think you're too young for this heavy work.'

"The redhead had been slowly turning white because of all the hayseed and ragwort seed that was in his hair and now he turned in desperation and pleaded with Father McFadden.

"'If you really want to help me, there's a spare pitchfork cause right now me father is under this load of hay.'".

"Where were we, gasson? Did you ever watch a child trying to conceal a beach ball under the water? The battalion was on top of a big roundy hill digging trenches in the middle of the night trying to keep themselves out of sight. If the child at the beach was very creative and if she managed to get a netted bag and howel the ball down under the water with the net by standing on the handles of the bag below the water, the child would still attract a lot of attention by the simple fact that he or she would be compelled to stay fixed in the same spot for a long period. It wasn't smart if you were trying to avoid attention."

Irish fishermen were compelled under fear of banishment, Paddy said, to smear their nets with oil and tar for 80 years before the artificial hunger in 1845, and this had the effect of scaring away the fish. Meanwhile the English fishermen were encouraged to preserve their nets with oak bark, which lasted two or three seasons and attracted the fish in huge numbers.

Crossmaglen in the early Seventies had an abundance of non-pedigree, untrained, stray dogs and more than a few bitches. The dogs observed one provincial unspoken rule, that of following backpacks and walkie-talkies.

"The non-pedigrees had trained themselves in the power of positive thinking: "Backpack-walkie-talkie, discarded bean tins with 15% of contents still intact – pass it on, Fido."

Paddy said he had it from a direct contact with Saint Bridget that the Cappy warrior knew a young maiden who had three dogs, and there was a preacher of Columcille prophecies in the Cappy Hills region who named the maiden "the doggie woman". This preacher said that Columcille predicted that there would come a time when there would be a dummy standing at every crossroads pointing out the way to go and there would be iron horses ploughing in the fields. Now these predictions have come to pass with signposts and tractors. The Cappy Hill region was sprinkled with young oaks and torn where the invading battalion was dug into their vantage point. They were using nets and oak leaves and all kinds of preservatives.

"The battalion must have intended to stay a long time." The Cappy warrior, watching the strangers trying to hide on top of Cappy Hill, was a bit like the child's audience at the beach. According to Paddy, "the Warrior was a light sleeper", and non-pedigree or not, he was a Jack Russell dog who could smell half-cooked beans in knapsacks miles away, especially if the wind was from the south and the strangers helicopter was shining a spotlight into every field in Cappy except Pete's Hill and the Hauckney Carraher's Hill. What was this terrible fixation with Cappy Hill?

Paddy's Saint Bridget contact told him the Warrior had an unanswered question: "It was kinda perplexin, even biblical like." The Cappy warrior had the same question the child's audience would have had, wondering why the child was staying in the same spot in the water. What was this fixation on the top of Cappy Hill that warranted this nightly attention?

Few scenes in life – nah, no visual or actual surroundings – can compare with the artistry natures employs in South Armagh in the first few weeks of the month of May each year. The Doggie Woman was free from homework and housework and Rex, her Jack Russell, was pawing at the door. The wind was blowing from the south into his small nostrils, foreign bean odours were in his nasal stream – Woof! 'Rex' led his troop down the boreen. The sun was high in the sky, Drumuckavall Hill loomed lofty in the east and beyond that was O'Nale's Castle in Glassdrummon. As Rex hung a right onto the mass pad which led to Drumboat. Slieve Gullion, home of McMurideth towered behind him. The older brother of the Doggie Woman cut a hazel rod from the hedge as the Warrior trod the pad [pathway] of the Lace-makers south. Saint Bridget's descendant told Paddy the warrior was reciting "The Spinners' Song".

*"Out comes the lad with the hazel*
*And the folding stars in the rack*
*Night's a good herd to the cattle*
*She sings, she brings all things back"*

There were roller-coaster panoramic views of sparsely soiled hills throughout the townlands of Cappy and Lissaraw in South Armagh which were created partly by glacier shifts.

"There were other role-players, the most significant being the real truth regarding the reason for the lack of soil on Cappy Rock, gasson, which was the fact that the English cut down all the giant oak trees and then the centuries of rainfall had resulted in exposing the nakedness of Cappy Rock".

"The late Malachy Conlon wrote a highly informative play entitled *Dunreavy No More* on the subject of the deforestation of this area. Where was I, gasson? Ah, yes. The Doggie Woman's younger sister was picking primroses by the gentle sloping banks of the stream dividing the townlands of Cappy and Lissaraw, Rex joined her for light refreshments, tadpoles burbled close by, the lad with the hazel opened the wooden gate which led through and across the Cais onto the mass pad and his younger brother was struggling behind. Half the Warrior's family were in Lissaraw and the lead group were across the townland border in Cappy.

"Townlands divided by a single fast flowing stream that flows to a wider stream, that becomes a river, that becomes the border, that divides and divides, and a hundred rivers are flowing between herself and her child."

Saint Bridget's descendant told Paddy that the Warrior said his primrose picker danced along the pad in the direction of Clonalig. She was the epitome of Celtic revival.

The townland of Clonalig was immediately below the high vantage point of Pete's Hill overlooking the site known as the Creggahwa. A line of an ancient poem ran through his head every time he was reminded of Clonalig; he said he had a next dure neighbour, a very saintly lady who always motivated him and encouraged him to keep on trying.

"'More power to you, Paddy,' she said, 'go on ye boy ye, build castles in the air.' She was Bridget Luckie and I loved her dearly," Paddy said.

*And with her I danced a gig*
*At the Creggahwa in Clonalig, Bridget said*

Birds sang, iron gates squeaked, loose stones fell on zestful, ditch-climbing youths living in the moment, drinking in the magnetic energy that makes South Armagh so unique. A three-day-old colt bolted closer to the piebald mare, a faced Suffolk yew, three lambs at foot emerged from within the ferns and torn maze which is Cappy, and she left particles of her outer fleece loosely hung upon the torn like a rising Egyptian mummy exiting her tomb. Saint Bridget's descendent told Paddy the Warrior related, a rabbit ran to its burrow, it had four legs".

Saint Bridget's descendent heard the Warrior reciting Paddy's skipping rhyme, "Ann, Ann, Ox, Ox" and chase the (two-legged) rabbits [the strangers] from Cappy Rock. The eldest lad with the hazel was at the site of the Famine Hamlet first. He stood a top of the remains of the bedroom window wall. Ragworts and briars carpeted the floors of the cabin, Nature had planted dandelion with honeysuckle as wallpaper midway up the bedroom walls. If only the Kirk family could smell this fragrance Paddy sighed.

Saint Bridget's descendent told Paddy that the Warrior related the story to his children regarding the historical importance and global contribution their starving ancestors had made to the world in the field of design arts and crafts. The Warrior was heard to say that there is on record in a private collection in New York a message in fine needlework, set in an oval frame and made by Anne Kirk when she was eight years old. Its title is "Live to Die".

*You whose few wishes to Heaven do aspire*
*Who made those Blessed abodes your sole desire*
*If you are wise and hope that blessed to gain*
*Use well your time, live not for wealth or gain*
*Let not the morrow your vain thoughts employ*
*But think this day the last you shall enjoy.*

A bunch of thyme bloomed on the cupboard shelf midway above where the settle bed would have stood, just left of the open hearth. Small particles of wild oats grew tall on the site of the fan bellows. The Warrior placed his left hand on the right shoulder of the lad with the hazel, and he began to sing.

> *Oh the violence began*
> *Near our home, Michael,*
> *When the strangers they came*
> *O'er the sea*
> *When I first set my eyes*
> *On your gaze, Michael,*
> *And my ears heard your*
> *First Celtic pleas*

Rex was barking feverishly, his hind legs cultivating the green grassy spring moss on the Kirk family hearthstone. Furiously he sneezed and barked. The Warrior's youngest bent down and retrieved a severed, four-leafed clover which Rex had elevated onto a petal of a wild Rose of Sharon's flower with his furious raking heels. "Grainnia Wail" (Ireland) sighed heavily and her sigh shook the fishing net above and around the battalion's trench on the Hauckney's Hill (nickname for Carragher). The Warrior exclaimed, "–And their sons will have sons as brave as were their fathers!"

Rex bolted west from Kirk's garden, and the Doggie Woman with her Rose of Sharon flower in hand followed; after all, Rex was her dog. She was the first of the Warrior's band in human form to witness the might of Rex as he checked out the oak bark preservatives on the foreign battalion's fishing net. Hauckney's Hill, Cappy, Crossmaglen, South Armagh, Ireland, a Jack Russell with no tail chasing two-legged rabbits away from Cappy Rock.

"Ann-Ann" – from the nursery rhyme – "couldn't do it a bit better herself," Paddy declared. "Terrified, misty brownish-eyed British soldiers peered out of polished, lathered faces, the brutal fishers of men, caught within their own nets, nets dependent on the remnants of Dunreavy Woods, woods fertilized by the decayed nets rotted by the tar and oils and tears and fears of the starving Celts."

By now they were by Cappy Lake, two miles south of Crossmaglen, which clapped its waters against the bull rushes and heather. Rex had no tail to wag, and the Doggie Woman hugged her Rose of Sharon while she studied its construction and unveiled its creative phases.

The Warrior looked down on the Cass-a-Cam first then further south to Cullen Grove. Tara Hill loomed in the horizon. Sixty foreign soldiers, who had been dug into a deep trench hoping to capture Irish Republican Volunteers, bundled the imported fishing nets they had cast out every day and night on the fertile ocean that is Crossmaglen, South Armagh. Fishers of men, casting their nets to no avail. They hauled them in empty, loaded up their jeeps then retreated, because they figured the Warrior might tip off other Republicans to ambush them.

In their moment of triumph, preserved forever in Paddy's imagination and in mine The Warrior stands on Celtic waters of hope, Rex holds his catch in his lenses, buries his surplus beans, leaps into the Warrior's arms with shamrocks on his beany nose. Then he leaps again, runs to the fairy bush, and on a trinity of legs he sheds a tear for Pearse, mustard seed for a burning bush. The sun tucks in behind Corris-Smoth, the retreated battalions in disarray. Cappy Hill belongs to Rex again.

"They tell me, gasson, that there's a book in Oxford University by the name of *Policraticus*; could you bate that? It has been required reading for the English to this present day. Now to tell you the truth, gasson, if these present eejits that's walking backways round Cross as I spake to you, if these boyos are up there in the big house on the Culloville road every night reading Chapter 21 of the aforementioned, pon me sowel, they'll make an awful mess of our unfortunes altogether, gasson."

Paddy took off his peaked cap and reached inside of it, never taking his eye off the fortified military post which commanded an overview of Cross Square. He thrust two typewritten pages into my hand. "Nawful pity I can't read, gasson," he said, shaking his head. These papers are very important "The schoolmasters in Shorts Snug predicted a very uncertain future for Cross based on the contents of the lining of me ould cap, gasson".

I was acutely conscious, judging by the tone of Paddy's voice, that it might be unwise to attract the sentry in the post by opening documents within his view.

"Pass no remarks of him!" Paddy assured me. "There's a slurry tanker pulling up outside of the Hole-in-Wall which will keep him occupied for a long time. Read away, gasson, you're as safe as a naked virgin on a building site in Cross the morning after the Rangers win the championship."

Then Paddy had a change of mind. He reached for his left shoulder strap; soon he would slip into one of his affirmations. Then he continued:

> *"Close they their ear*
> *With cotton wool of fear*
> *Whistlen with borrowed wind*
> *"Halt" their nation's sins'.*

Paddy said Pauderdeen taught him that from the Good Book. Paddy said, then he was reciting again

> *And he showed me a pure river of water of life*
> *Clear as crystal*
> *Proceeding out of the throne of God and of the lamb*
> *In the midst of the street of it*
> *And on either side of the river*
> *Was there the tree of life*
> *Which bare twelve manner of fruit*
> *And yield her fruit every month*
> *And the leaves of the tree*
> *Were for the healing*
> *Of the nations*

# Agro

"Now I'll just tell you, gasson," Paddy said as he converted the evening stroll of two spiders into a swim in a tobacco-polluted pool, "there's them smart boyos round these parts with high flutin' names, gasson, and they be laughing at the way we spake here. Pon me sowel, maybe it's them that could learn a thing or two if they'd come to Cross for the ould craic.

"There was a boyo be the name of Willy Morris who wrote a book a few years ago explaining all about alphabets. Wouldn't it bate the divil if yer man Morris the very man that towel the world about their Indo-European roots, had relatives round Cross? Morris explained in great detail where we all came from and he towel the craic about all this 'agro' that's happening in Cross at this minute as I spake, gasson.

"That Morris reckoned that word or root had been anglicized over 6000 years from its Indo-European form 'agro'. It was first changed to 'akraz', then it was changed again to 'accer' then it got changed again to 'acre'. Willy Morris also showed how the Celtic and Gaelic languages come from a prehistoric source as yet unidentified when Morris towel the ould craic in 1970, when he wrote his book. Wouldn't it be some craic if it turned out that the prehistoric proto- Indo- European source turned out to be a Mass rock or a Hedgerow school in the Baroney of the Fews in South Armagh.

Pon me sowel, and stranger things have happened, gasson. You think am codding you, don't you? Well them schoolmasters in Shorts Snug showed me pictures of the Celtic language before the 'split with the bryths'. They towel me the Irish and the Scottish went the Goid route; while the Cornish and the Welsh went with the bryths. Mind you, gasson, I only know what I saw in the pictures, the writing on page 363 of the American Heritage Dictionary meant nothing to me except what the schoolmasters towel me. Didn't it bate the divil the way the word 'agro' got kicked about? There was plenty of 'agro' round Cross of the non-agricultural type, avick."

"As a Crossmaglen man," Paddy continued, "I don't care how much people know – until I know how much people care.

"Did I tell you the craic about the strangers flying about in their helicopter? Apparently these strangers are looking for some more of those ancient burial stones that South Armagh is famous for. The stones they have in Stonehenge came originally from Cappy and Coolderry and Clarnagh in South Armagh. That was during the time of the full growth in Dunreavy Wood."

# Tug-o-war

"There's another craic I heard one night," Paddy went on. "I was doing a bit of fishing under Larkin's Bridge – you never know what you'll catch up that country, avick. There was two men covering pits of praties alongside of the Creggan river, one of them was very fond of breastfeeding his long-handled spade".

MAN AT WORK

"I heard them spake
The ould men heavy on the sod
Letting their angers come
Between them and the thought of God
Old men complaining"

"From what I could catch, in between catching a bad dose of a cowl, it appears that one evening the strangers flew up over the 'five towns' on the other side of the invisible partition across Ireland. There was a big Kerryman out at the Coffin Bridge one side of Dundalk; he was keeping an eye on a busy farmyard entrance that was leading onto the broad road. He belonged to the Irish Garda Your man took off his cap and blessed himself when he saw the helicopter crash-landing in a field near Roache Castle. Well, be God, didn't it turn out that the Shelagh tug-o-war team just happened to be training under one of the big ash trees in the same area, pon me sowel, gasson, and weren't the Shelagh boys pulling a couple of creamery cans of artificial fertilizer up and down the ash tree with a big heavy rope.

"It's a holy terror the way things happen sometimes, gasson, ye think I'm codding ye. The Shelagh lads were that dumbfounded when they saw the helicopter over their heads – you know the way you would be yourself, gasson, when something extraordinary happened; you would forget all about what you were doing beforehand – and the Shelagh lads got that mesmerized, they let go the bloody rope that was tied to the two creamery cans filled with artificial fertilizer and according to the boyo that was breastfeeding the spade, there was a few pieces of horse shoes and frost nails and harrow pins and things like that to make up the weight.

"The creamery cans headed off for the briars and nettles at the foot of the ash tree faster than Newton's apple. It wouldn't happen again in a month of Sundays, but what was lying at the foot of the ash tree in among the roots and gillgowns and ragworts, but an ould turnip barrow. Pon me sowel it was lying there that long that nobody knew about it, and when the creamery cans hit the turnip barrow, it struck it with such an almighty 'scud' that the bloody barrow rose up out of the nettles and took off like a rocket, gasson, and be the lomity God, gasson, didn't the tug-o-war team do the only sensible thing they could – they ran for the nearest derelict house in County Louth. As for the bloody eejits in the helicopter, they had that much polish on their faces and with the heat of the engine, didn't it start to melt, and the polish ran into their eyes and not one of them could read the bloody map.

"The turnip barrow took flight for the thingamajig of a helicopter in the sky that was carrying the bakers' dozen of strangers who couldn't read the map."

heard it from Paddy Dan Bugs' [Paddy's Loye] gersa that the roller of the turnip barrow got caught in the propeller of the helicopter and the next thing the gersa towel me she saw was the lid flying off the vessel that howls the turnip seed in the barrow. Could you believe that, avick? Now bear in mind the gersa was a young slip of a thing with good eyesight – not like meself, gasson. The gersa swore she saw it with her own two eyes: a handful of turnip seeds that was still lying in the bottom of the vessel, they spilled, that she heard it at a skittle game at a crossroads somewhere, they spilled into the petrol tank of the helicopter, and be God, gasson, didn't the engine begin to flutter and fart, and the next there was smoke coming out of the back dure of it, gasson, and what do you think happened next?

## THE WESSEX HELECOPTER

"Paddy Dan Bug's gersa towel me the boyos with the inability of reading the maps, what did they do, gasson, but started to fire big bullets with flames coming out of them at the unfortunate small farmers in the derelict house who were after being forced to abandon their tug-o-war practise. These flaming bullets landed on the thatch roof in the ould shed in Biddy the Nailer's Haggard, and in the meantime the engine of the helicopter was beginning to sound like Meegan's ould thrasher long ago. The helicopter was losing air rights faster than Newton's apple. Law of Relations or no law of relations, the tug-o-war team agreed to a man that evening that what goes up over the Five Towns in the Barony of the Fews, must be brought down."

The gersa told Paddy she heard the captain of the tug-o-war team saying that they wouldn't be depending on Newton's law, either.

The gersa heard it at a skittle game at a crossroads somewhere between Clarnagh and Carron Hill that the helicopter finished up in a boggy marsh one side of Dundalk, and the Shucky Kauny broke two spokes in the back wheel of his bike and one spring in the saddle trying to find it.

"The weemens of the farmhouse," where he had been directing silage hauling Ferguson tractors outside the gate, "had two, big, earthen crocks of tay made and they had half a churn of buttermilk watered down with spring water. They had to throw the whole lot out cause every man jack about the haggard that had been working at the silage, they were away like a shot over the road with tractors and tedders and strong ropes."

Every small farmer was out in the Marshes with tractors and they were fighting over which one would get the propellers of the helicopter.

"Great yokes for drying roundy bales, gasson!" Paddy said. "The tug-o-war training tactics of the Shellagh team were changed after that evening for ever more. There was good anchor men on both sides of the rope when the heavyset man shouted, 'Pick up the slack'." Isn't it a holy terror, gasson, how simple a dirty row can start all over a bit of craic with creamery cans and an ould turnip barrow an a bin. Me sowel, if them other eejits had to be able to read the bloody maps! What the hell were they doing with the maps in the first place if they couldn't read them? Shure there's no need to be laughing at me here at the Barrack Corner with me ould newspaper upside down! Pon me sowel, if they come pointing their fingers at me and if they take me for a fool, they'll be only too glad to lave me back."

# The Rectangle Square

"Crossmaglen, where the Square is a rectangle," Paddy mused one day. "And you'd be for asking me, gasson, who do we think we are? The world appears mystified as to why I haven't bothered to copy the English habit of recording messages onto paper, or for that matter why am never pressured into taking English messages or instructions off papers, either. It went against every principle of my Druidical way of life, pon me sowel, I got this far without the scribble, gasson, and I'll get another bit with me ancient methods.

"W. B. Yeats fully understood what was moving within himself; Yeats could figure out the melody that jumps about through me ould head, gasson. Yeats once wrote to a friend explaining the Oriental significance of Ireland. Did I tell you the craic about the way the Orientals completely missed the Wicked Sister's island on their way to us and they stopped with us for years, and they brought back our Celtic music when they were leaving? The Orientals left plenty of gassons and gersas on the island of Ireland, pon me sowel. Yeats had it well sussed out when he wrote to Gitanjali back there in 1912 regarding their singing:

*"Yer lyrics, display in their thought, a world I have dreamed about all my life, a tradition where poetry and religion are the same thing, has passed through the centuries, gathering from learned and unlearned metaphor and emotion and carried back again to the multitude. A whole people, a whole civilization, seems to have been taken up into this imagination and we are moved because we have met our own image, or heard, perhaps for the first time, our voice as in a dream, the cry of the flesh and the cry of the soul seem one.*

### *AN EXILE'S DREAM*
*"I did arise – an I went there*
*And I prayed that Cross I'd see*
*I vowed – clay and wattle seized there*
*From clutch of queen I'd free*
*"Oh when we are up – we are up*
*And when we are down – we'll not frown*
*But when we are only halfway up*
*We're still ahead of the crown."*

103

# Crosseology'

"Did the prince send ye, gasson?" Paddy said, eyeing me warily as he converted my torso to a vertical wind-breaker for the momentary purposes of lighting his Peterson tobacco pipe.

I was thinking perhaps Paddy might be screening me as a possible 'spy'.

"We don't spake to strangers here, gasson," he said in between puffs and drags of tobacco. Paddy smokes the same tobacco that he chews. In 1971 Carroll's No. 1 tobacco was made in Carroll's Factory in Dundalk, Ireland.

"Bejazzus, we spake to no strangers." Paddy was standing upright now, hazel stick in hand. He drummed it off his Wellington boot leg. The sound travelled round the Square in like fashion to an African bongo drum. Paddy raised the hazel cane and placed it across his shoulder blades with both hands placed at either ends, somewhat resembling a tribesman holding his Kualay staff of authority. Paddy was studying me to ensure I had not come from some other foreign place..

"No connection with royalty, Paddy," I interjected in an effort to dispel his fears that I might be acting on behalf of the commanding officer of a parachute regiment in a foreign country.

Paddy's question about the prince was running through my head. What could it mean?

"Are ye sure this prince what's-his-name didn't send you?" Paddy demanded, as if reading my thoughts.."

"Boris something or other is his name. The whole craic round these parts about five or six years ago, gasson, was that there was a bunch of boyos studying ethnology, archaeology and Egyptology. I was thinking, gasson, when I seen you coming out of that taxi, that maybe you belonged to that bunch an maybe you were going to start some sort of scientific probe be the name of 'Crosseology'."

Paddy was fixing a couple of bachelor buttons on his waistcoat one night in Shorts Snug he said when the schoolmasters were receiving some hot refreshments in the form of the contents of the boiling kettle .

"There was a lot of talk about the 'continuing quest for knowledge'," Paddy recalled. "There was also a lot of talk about yer man Edmund Hilary who they said tested man's endurance an reaction to the thin cowl air at the top of the world."

Paddy was wondering how long Hilary would stick it at the Barrack Corner in Crosse. It seemed that one of the schoolmasters had a cousin in America and this fellow sent him a copy of a report prepared by a Chicago daily news writer.

"His name was George Weller, and he had a Pulitzer Prize on his desk. This boyo George says that there's a race of people in Africa who are known by the name of the Fuzzy-Wuzzies. The Fuzzy-Wuzzies fought the British along the Nile in the days of Mohammed Ahmed – fierce guerrillas."

One of the schoolmasters was reading out of a handful of loose pages in his hand and Paddy got a glimpse of a picture on one of the pages the master left down between the plate of sliced lemons and the sugar bowl on the table. He caught the outline of a man's face on the picture through the veil of steam which was rising out of the three glasses on the south side of the table.

"Pon me sowel, gasson, whatever was in the ould kettle, it was greatly assisting the master in his fluency of words. He was wondering if his ould kettle could ever be converted into some sort of an 'Aladdin's Genie' with powers and if it would be able to accomplish the same results as what he was witnessing in the snug that night. The face in the picture had a sharp, pointed nose and lean cheeks; the eyes were intense, the lips pressed firmly together. The hair on the head of the male warrior was ragged, tossed, in an upright standing manner. It had an unkempt appearance similar to that I have seen on Cross youths and fathers coming back from the disused mill in Bessbrook after spending a week in confinement." Just then the front door opened and in stepped three British soldiers, members of a foot patrol, they commenced to check the id's of all the customers and when they came to paddy and myself they told us we were under arrest for suspicious behaviour. we were roughly sezied and marched off to the barracks where my rucksack was searched and all my personal papers laid out on the desk including a letter from my girlfriend which they handed around for all to read. i was asked several questions as to my visit in crossmaglen to which i replied i was looking for work. paddy on the other hand was amusing himself with the goats langle and making all kinds of weird gestures at the soldiers letting them think he was crazy.. After about  half hour we were allowed to go back to Shorts bar to continue our socializing.

"Prince Boris De Rachewiltz was your man's name," Paddy recalled. "Them smugglers, according to the masters in Shorts Snug – now, you're sure he didn't send ye, gasson?" Paddy looked at me hard. "But then again, gasson, he wouldn't have the gall.

"These learned brethren in the snug were discussing the merits of words like 'individual' and 'independence' and independent'. "It was Indo this and Indo that. That spake, gasson, 'he wouldn't have the gall', goes back thousands of years. But I was telling you about Weller and the Prince fella who spent a whole winter poking through ould meat markets in Cairo studying camel herders and smugglers. Them smugglers according to what I heard in between spoon stirring and kettle pouring and Saracen roaring bouts in the snug, them smugglers in the masters' papers weren't allowed to carry arms – not legally, anyway."

I couldn't help wondering where Paddy was going with this diversion about a little-known African tribe which, for the life of me, the prince and Weller were studying. My span in Crossmaglen was all of 50 minutes old but I was maturing rapidly – or was it a case of 'second time round'? Has that ever happened to you?  You arrive in a far distant land for the first time only to discover your surroundings are vaguely familiar. Here I was in the ancient 'Barony of the Fews' or the 'Oriel of ould'.  I thought about that, too, for a while. I was remembering a connection or perhaps the origins of a Celtic race; could there be a connection?

Paddy had earlier said that the Euro in European owed its origin to the original name for the island of Ireland. Euro has been anglicised down to Eire. Whenever Tom Conner (a Culloville man married to Paddy's Aunt) would be in the middle of a craic he would always refer to the Bejazz-us

Paddy said, "I was only a slip of a gasson meself at the time, gasson, but I remember it just the same as if it was yesterday, Tom would always re-affirm the comparison of the little-known African tribe which the Prince and Weller were studying, according to what the masters were reading out of the Chicago report. It was only when listening to the schoolmaster's artful reading describing the experiences of the Prince and Weller in their attempts to trace the pre-dynastic Egyptians that I realized how similar their situation was to our own. Of course, I cannot confirm the truth or otherwise of what I heard, gasson, that is to say, it wasn't for the want of opportunity or lack of material. No, it was all there in front of me on the table."

I figured it was not Paddy's eyesight that was the problem; could it be that Paddy couldn't read English?

"Not a bliddy word of it, gasson, just the pictures."

# Literary Genius

My dad had told me about the early exploits of Paudric Colum round the roads of Cavan. Dad said Colum wrote a poem one time which contained the line, 'out comes the lad with the haze'. Dad was tapping into the space between my ears again now.

"They are expert fishers of men round Cross," he had warned, "you will never see their line and they change bait in mid-air, and as for their rods, well!"

Padraic Colum was a very famous poet. He was a Longford man, and used to spend a lot of time with his uncle Mick Reilly round the roads of Cavan.

## PADRAIC COLUM

"Padraic Colum was the poet's name," Dad said. Now, I knew from the fireside stories of my granddad that the fowl dalers from Crossmaglen were at that same time, the early 1900's, famous all over Ireland for their expertise in survival skills and comradery.

I was recalling some lines of the popular ballad recorded in whose memory, "The Dalin Men from Crossmaglen". Padraic Colum used to recite and compose some of his poetry and folklore stories on the side of the road around Shercock and Beilebouragh, and whenever young Paudric's Uncle Mick was engaged in examining the contents of the Cross pony and traps full of fowl, "Young Padraic was subjected to much laughter and storytelling and stick waving and hand clapping and hand slapping and debates about luck-pennies."

Colum's world-famous poem 'A Drover' was composed from experiences young Padraic had witnessed crossing Mulligan's Kesh with the dalin men from Crossmaglen.

"Did I tell you the craic about smuggling the County Meath cattle every first Thursday in the month across Mulligan's Kesh for Crosse Fair the next day, gasson? Well if I didn't then I will later, but where was I anyway? I lost me train of thought. Oh yes, have it now: 'A Drover'."

He began to recite:

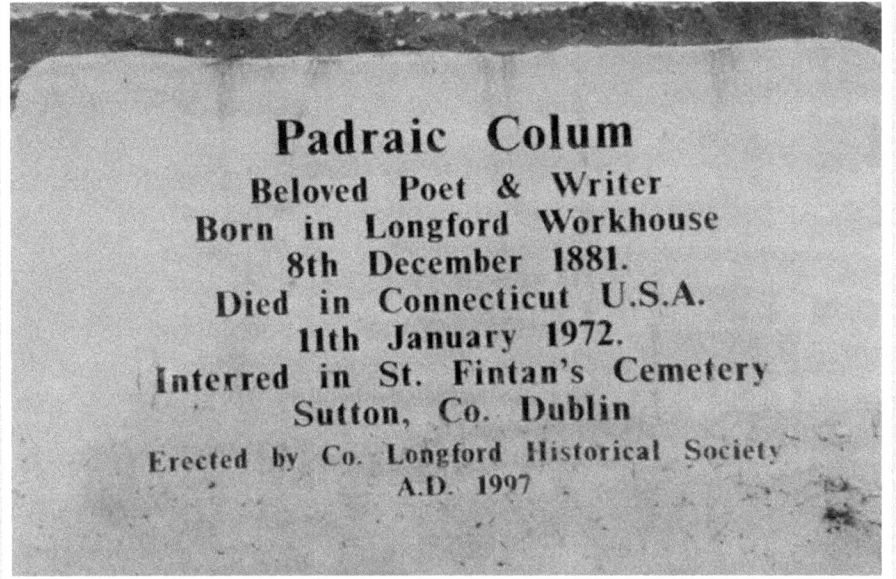

**LONGFORD MEMORIAL STONE**

*"To Meath of the pastures*
*From wet hills by the sea*
*Through Leitrim and Longford*
*Go my cattle and me."*

("The next bit is where he swung a left at Federna Bush.")

*"Then the wet, winding roads*
*Brown bogs with water*
*And my thoughts on white ships*
*And the king of Spain's daughter."*

"The next place is even more
Interesting for 'Crosse'."

*"And the crowds at the 'Fair'*
*The herds loosened and blind*
*Loud words and dark faces*
*And the wild blood behind."*

"It's a funny ould thing the way things turn about too, gasson. Pon me sowel, it's a long road there's no turn on. They tell me, gasson, that James Joyce " – or "Jice" as Paddy pronounced it – "they tell me that Jice gave Colum's poem "A Drover" a mention in *Ulysses*. Doesn't that take the biscuit, gasson? Maybe you could help prove that the Crosse dalin men were responsible for inspiring literary genius in Joyce and Colum. There's a couple of pints in it for yourself if you pull that one off. They'll all be wishing and claiming they were born in Cross then."

"There's another twist put in the tail of the divil round Cross," Paddy continued according to the schoolmasters in Shorts Snug, Colum was married to a woman be the name of McGuire – there's plinty of that name around Crosse, they have been in this parish of Upper Creggan for centuries. They tell me that their ancestors was the subject of a famous poem written during the 'Artificial Hunger'."

Paddy said he had heard his father reciting it many a time, but he could only remember bits of it now. "They might come to me later," he said cheerfully.

**"The Goatman from Coothehill:**
"T'was in the month of March
And the Fane was in a swill
Shure I took them home by Lissaraw
And on through Cullovillle
And I bought them off
The brock McGuire in the town of Crossmaglen
And I drank me fill
And I'd do the same again
Said the "Goatman from Cootehill"
They were teddered in a haggard
T'was by John Aisy's Hill
And am heartily glad I met McGuire
Cause by God they're milking still.

Paddy said, There are descendants of 'McGuire' about these hills and fields round Crosse yet, and pon me sowel, gasson, as good a bit of craic as you could meet in a day's walking or fishing for that matter. Where were we, gasson? It's time to get off the long-acre in Cavan. "Padraic Colum was born on December 8th, 1881, round about the same time as the McQuillan sisters were teaching the 'Carrickmacross Lace' over there where the milkman McShane is living now on the Square.

"Did I tell you about the lacework patterns designed around the ancient love knot of Ireland, gasson? Did I tell you the craic about the ancient monks coming inland to the Barony of the Fews when the monasteries were being plundered in the early centuries, gasson? You're the scholar, you have letters after your name, study this one, gasson. You were looking for work, isn't that what I heard you saying, gasson? There you have it now: There's a slip of an Irish country, gasson, with a grandmother by the name of Connelly and a grandfather by the name McCormack."

Paddy was really warming up now. He had both hands on either side of where he sat on his windowsill, and he was leaning the full force of his upper body onto his palms. This action caused his shoulders to become raised. His lower body became lucid, his legs began to swing and he clicked his boot heels together in repeated fashion.

"Am telling you, gasson – it's a long road there's no turn on." He looked out towards Glassdrummin Castle in the east. "There you have the world reading about the Dalin men from Crossmaglen in Joyce's *Ulysses*, and you have Padraic Colum's experience with the Saxon Shilling, which they tell me relates to a young Irishman who joined an army in Britain.

"Colum's story describes how this (now) British soldier confronts his sister to defend his actions in joining the British army, only to learn that his father had been taken prisoner by the Brits and his sister is all alone to defend their ancestral home. The new Brit in Colum's story remembered his Irishness and picked up his father's gun to march out of the house to confront the eviction party

"The Brits killed him on the spot!"

It was interesting to reflect back on the fact that a literary genius, Padraic Colum, who had penned the line, "We can't buy ourselves back with the money we sold ourselves out for", was a direct descendant of Saint

Columbkille. It was indeed worthy of some thought that Colum should have gotten the most of his youthful inspiration and most if not all of the material for his stories from the Dalin men from Crossmaglen.

"Mark my words, gasson, Colum wrote them words in 1901. I think it was Oct 28th. Am not sure …but here we are now in Crosse and it's 1971 and this is the very same spot where Colum stood on with his uncle Micky Burns, and I have it on good authority that there was manys the cartload of fowl changed hands right here at the Barrack Corner in Crosse between that same Micky Burns and the Dalin men from Crosse.

"Micky Burns would always be the seller. The fowl plucking industry was thriving in Crosse at that time Colum would have been a teenager then; this is before he went to Dublin to start to get more material from Padraig Pearce and Thomas McDonagh. Colum's then-girlfriend, soon to be his wife, was teaching in Pearce's school, St Edna's, then the Colum's went to America in 1914."

Paddy was clicking his heels again. "You said it was work you were looking for."

I nodded; there wasn't much else I could do.

"But before Colum left," Paddy continued, "he gave Arthur Griffith's lads a hand to unload a boatful of rifles in Howth. And everybody's asking me where this road will take you to, as he pointed out the Culloville Road which leads to Monaghan, and thence onto Cavan."

"I must confess to a slight curiosity myself, Paddy," I said. (Did you notice I was practising my green horning there?).

Paddy looked at me with a certain amount of polite misgivings, but I had avoided asking the question, so he grudgingly acknowledged the fact.

"Well, at least you're trying, gasson. Try it with a bit of saliva on the top of your tonsils the next time. Well, all I know is that it's out that road young Colum went with his uncle Micky Burns, and of course Burns had with him a pocket full of white fivers from the Dalin men from Crossmaglen."

# Crossmaglen Fowl Market
# at the Barrack Corner

ffffff

"You know, it mighten be that much of an accident that Colum became personal friends with Thomas McDonagh, one of the signatories of the proclamation, gasson, but that's not here nor there in relation to your interest regarding where the Culloville road in Crosse will lead you. You can start from here, gasson, and go to any heights imaginable in this ould world, provided, of course, you start by using your imagination in the first place."

That's the way Paddy is: 'pragmatic' Paddy has a sort of 'trans-mutational' mechanism very Celtic, diverse, Paddy can fuse multiple topics into a kind of 'seasonal hybrid' without effort. Paddy can 'circus juggle' many subjects while his eye remains scanning passing pedestrians and traffic of varying dimensions, colour and size. Paddy can leave his topics afloat as it were in mid-air, enter into a new topic or topics of contrasting vein, and still maintain focus and contact with his original train of thought!

"Where was I, gasson? oh yeah. Colum never quit till he landed on the stage in Carnegie Hall, gasson, and then they made him the Dean of Columbia University. And you're standing there wondering where the Culloville road in Cross will lead you to."

At this point I was wishing my Dad's voice would come in over the airwaves. How many levels were there to this green horning concept? Did Paddy belong to a Bardic Society? Why was I finding so much work? How come nobody else was picking up this challenge?

"Are you still with me, gasson? How is that bit of lead howling out? Did you bring enough with you? Visionaries, poets forming Irish Theatre, becoming world famous, exiled in 1914, memories and stories with him from Crossmaglen about red-haired youths becoming 'Old Soldiers'."

# Celtic Riddle Talk

Paddy is in all aspects your true Celt. His conversation is in riddle formation.

"Catch it if you can; its name is 'Tain' and Paddy's your man. We were talking there earlier about the Bejas. To be straight with you, am going back now to my learned friends in the Shorts Snug for you, gasson. I have a bit of a problem trying to figure this whole thing out meself, gasson. There's me at the Barrack Corner all domesticated with me gaberdine coat and me four horse nails and a cobbler's auger, and in between stories about 'Bull Calf' smuggling via Herculean cyclists from the scholarly gathering in the Snug."

Paddy began to get the gist of what this Prince Boris and your man Weller had uncovered in Africa, but it raised some questions which had their origin somewhere close to "the peak of me ould cap". They didn't settle there too long. His questions soon made their way into the swill of his tobacco chaw, where he proceeded to fine-tune them before releasing them to his unsuspecting but pleasantly jovial assembled historians.

Paddy's first question caused his three scholarly friends to enter into an immediate, low-key consultation in the corner. The result of this 30-second brainstorming session was the summoning up of the proprietor for a refill of John Powers. The leader of the barnstormers then requested that a fourth member should join their group at the table. The proprietor was a bit of an historian himself but as he was engaged in a Gaelic Football debate in the other room, he declined the offer and he summoned the lady of the house to bring the bottle of Powers to the snug for the task at hand.

"I think the schoolmasters were employing the 'Dia-a-Crosse-tic' approach," Paddy said.

Paddy employed the four most widely used words in the English language whenever he was faced with stiff, unanswered questions, as Paddy called it. Where was I, reader? Now I'm starting to sound like Paddy! That can happen to you also in Crossmaglen; lots of changes can and will occur to your person in Crossmaglen. Most prominent will be your tendency to develop frequent mild discomforts around your rib cage and lower tummy muscles. This you can put down to the almost continuous igniting of your inbuilt laughter mechanism.

"I was telling you about the four most used words I employ, gasson. I have one for each of the 'Shan Van Vocht' green fields. The words are: *of, to, and, ahh.*

"I might not be able to read or write, gasson, but I have developed a very sophisticated method of counting. I use the 32 counties of Ireland when I need to count, gasson. Can I get the lend of your pencil, gasson, for a wee minute?"

"Sure, Paddy", I said, handing it over.

He began to convert my full-length pencil to a pipe cleaner by use of his penknife round its middle in such a manner as to ensure we both were equally equipped with writing utensils, as Paddy described them.

"Thraught n' a bin me sowel,(indeed upon my soul) gasson, I'll not be competing in the same arena as yourself for the work at hand, but you were looking for work, isn't that what I heard you saying?" He proceeded to let the sunlight onto the lead of his newly acquired half of my No. 2 HB pencil. "I can see you're wondering about the sugar and cloves and the lemons and boiling water, gasson. I suppose you're thinking there's another connection there with the four provinces of the island we're standing upon? And then there was John Power; where does he fit in?"

Paddy had now succeeded in extracting the entire wood casing from around the lead of his half of what had been until then my pencil. He had the thin fine line of pencil lead converted into a pipe cleaner as he spoke: "That's more like it, gasson." Then he replaced the punctured "Guinness" bottle top over his newly lighted pipe. "I was beginning to feel like 'Oweine and the Daws' there, gasson. Did I tell you the craic about the stuffing of Owiene's chimney by the daws? Unlucky ould work; I'll tell you about it again. Where were we, anyway? Be dads, I have it now, me questions to the masters. There used to be five provinces in Ireland, before I leave me craic about John Powers. Meath was the fifth one, gasson, but then there's five towns in this parish that certain among us would have you believe they were in another country, but I'll tell you about that one later."

I put it down to an absence of front teeth because I began to notice the occasional excited tremble, or perhaps it was caused by an overload of ashes, then again it might have been the build-up of enthusiasm which Paddy was frequently seen to exude, but for whatever of this trilogy of reasons, Paddy's blazing crooked shank pipe would regularly take on the appearance of a water diviner's stick in that it physically began to dance while Paddy maintained words, jaws, head and hand movements.

"Eye hath not seen, nor ear heard the plan behind the smokescreen of a Crossmaglen pipe smoker.". That's what my Dad told me; boy oh boy, will I ever conquer this "green-horning"? There was no point in quoting Churchill to Paddy. Never ever quit, Churchill said, but then I was as well saying it as thinking it, because Paddy could read minds.

"So what was the point in learning to read books, gasson, when I know what's going into them before it hits the paper, gasson, pon me sowel."

"Paddy, I'll not argue that one atall, atall."

I was well enough pleased with my first attempt – well, actually it slipped out; I was kind of startled!

"Can you pick praties, gasson?"

Paddy viewed my astonished expression – I had never even witnessed a potato harvesting operation.

"Do you know, gasson, that an empty sack won't stand? I have a handful of Kerr's Pink praties in a saucepan on the back of the doric cooker, gasson, and a few laves of Barley Hill curly cabbage draped over them to keep the steam close to their skin." He said the cabbage leaves would encourage the praties to take off their skins a bit quicker – "and an empty sack won't stand, gasson."

I was remembering stories from my grandfather in relation to the various species of potatoes grown in Ireland. Could it be that Paddy was possibly referring to an upcoming meal of cooked potatoes, perhaps? Maybe I would qualify for this 'Crosse-over-tin-Tology', as Paddy described it. Yet, just maybe –

"Yer learning, gasson", Paddy said as he ran his fingers through his hair, alternating the strokes between spits onto his palms/ "Fuzzy-Wuzzies – Bejas – well, when you have the name of early rising, you can lie till dinnertime, that's provided, of course, they don't come and break down your dure in the middle of the night, gasson. Did I tell you about the quare fellow across the shuck, gasson? Bejas, we will need to keep an eye on them, according to the craics I've been hearing round about Shorts Snug lately!"

Paddy continued, "It's worse than fierce the kind of shenanigans they are planning for Crosse this few years. There's a boyo over in England drawing pictures of a pack of cards on a clothesline. Did you ever hear the beating of that?"

I picked up the large box of Swan matches next to Paddy's Woodbine pack on his Barrack Corner massive stone structure which made up the original site of the first dwelling that was later to become Lennon's Crossroads and eventually Lennon's Alehouse until it finally became Crossmaglen.

I agreed to assist Paddy in all areas of enlightenment. After all, I needed the work, and striking Swan matches for a Woodbine smoker on a winter's evening at the Barrack Corner in Crosse is hard work, but while Paddy and I were engaged in intimate hand touching endeavours which in other cultural circles might be misinterpreted – Paddy with his coat over his head and me in celebrant pose with cupped hands holding the burnt offering – I'm getting the hang of this Celtic riddle talk; what do you think, reader? My eagerness to engage in this smoke-ring signalling bout was solely for the purpose of engaging Paddy's windpipe in-activities which excluded speaking while Paddy was "inhaling mouthfuls of east wind from Russia", as he put it.

I had a chance to think out loud, so to speak – sure would love to see the design of that 'Billy-cycle' – woodpeckers with electronic eyes.

"Beats me, Paddy."

"Ah for God's sake, gasson, that's not the half of it. Apparently, this boyo be the name of Emmet designed a thingamajig with a woman's brain and he gave her the name Tizzy. It was a robot for defusing roadside landmines. But no matter one way or the other, these schoolmasters got me ould goat up when they towel me this Emmet fella employed Celtic designs of serpents and things and into the bargain, spools of thread, lamp stands, spark plugs, oil cans and bits of pratie diggers to make a contraption for carrying Kosan gas cylinders and creamery cans away from roadside shucks and empty houses around Crosse. Could you believe that, gasson? What do you make of it all? These boyos are expecting me to believe this Emmet fella's machine can ate buns and drink minerals. Well, we'll need to watch this Emmet fella whenever he arrives in Crosse with this Tizzy-Lizzy yoke to try and change us, gasson."

"Will you stick it, gasson? The work I mane, are you up till it? I hope so, Nawful pity Colum is dead, gasson, Lord rest his soul. to think he left from the Barrack Corner in Crosse and finished up an Honorary Doctorate of Columbia University in New York – bates all, pon me sowel, that Padraic Colum was a direct descendant of Saint Columbkille and he found himself teaching in the Philosophy department of Columbia University in 1958—wonder was he teaching the 'Philosophy of Crossmaglen', gasson."

> "But close to the ground are reared
> The wings that have the widest sway
> And the birds that sing best in the woods
> Were reared with breasts to the clay

> Padraic Colum

> "Crossmaglen, I love you
> You're the pillow of my dreams
> Your soil I'll wear beneath my nails
> I'll wash them in your streams."

> Patrick McEntegart

Paddy gazed with turbulent fountains of multi-coloured domes lighted by an inner concealed energy which appeared to pump the warm liquid over their brim occasionally as in a Manhattan hotel foyer – the surplus would someday return to its source within. His eyes rested on 'Crossmaglen's Faceless Clock'.

"Did I tell you the craic about the landlord 'Ball', gasson? That was the boyo that the townland Ballsmill was named after. Pon me sowel and it's time it was changed. What would be wrong with calling it 'Bradford' in memory of the Glassdrummon Protestant who was publicly scourged by the British yeomen for giving his mass house to the Catholics? We'd be better off remembering Bradford and eliminating the name of a shameful landlord who insulted the people of Crossmaglen by deliberately erecting a dummy clock face on the market house for all to see."

# Honolulu

"Were you ever in Honolulu, gasson?" Paddy asked as he blew hard down his right nostril, while his left one remained tightly closed from the pressure of his right thumb. He rubbed his eyes with the inside lining of his cap at the same time. I got the impression the nose-blowing was perhaps a diversion to shield attention away from the eyes.

"Where was I, gasson, with me ould craic?"

"Honolulu, Paddy."

"Right, me flower, try this one on for size, gasson. Maybe I should give you back that pencil lead, gasson." Paddy's eyes were brighter now. "I think it was about 1922 or 3, somewhere around that period, anyway." The Hawaiian government were looking for somebody to gather up stories, legends, poems, and that kind of stuff to teach in their national schools. "The legislature couldn't get a living soul high up or low down until they contacted Padraic Colum." The bold Colum landed in a cottage in Waikiki, hung a cartwheel of flowers over his neck like an ass's collar and headed up the middle of the town and into the library and started looking for Polynesian records.

"It wouldn't happen again not in a month of Sundays and only a boyo well versed in the apprenticeship of fowl-plucking would spot what Colum saw next, gasson."

Paddy said he had it from high authority that Colum started humming 'The Dalin Men from Crossmaglen' the minute he saw the head honcho of Honolulu coming towards him down the street.

"Your man was wearing a shawl made out of birds' feathers – white ones, yellow ones, red ones – and the interesting difference Colum immediately noticed between the Waikikians and the Crosse-o-pluckins", Paddy said, "was the Honoluans were only allowed to pluck one feather out of a bird and then let it go for another twenty years. Colum knew that the boys round Crosse wouldn't wait twenty years to pluck fowl – twenty minutes would be more like it."

Whatever Colum found in the libraries and museums in Honolua, he was lecturing to the Hawaiian Academy within a couple of months.

"Ye know, gasson, ye have to hand it to the Longford boyos sometimes, but it took the 'Fowl Dalers from Crosse' to teach them their apprenticeship. You were looking for work," he continued. "Well, I'll not keep a good man down."

It was smoke signalling time again, as Paddy described it, and pencil sharpening time for me.

"Did I tell you Colum was a direct descendent of Saint Columbkille?"

Paddy was onto one of his Bardic rolls again; he seemed to enjoy talking about the Columbkille prophecies. What was it about Paddy or Crossmaglen or the Barony of the Fews – how come the governments of the world had failed to recognise this vast culture? What would an International Impact Assessment Study unveil here? Why not an expedition?

"Howel on there, gasson, them's my questions you're tossing about in your head!"

Paddy was waving the brown index finger on his left hand. The colouring resembled that of Padraic Colum's associates in Honolua in the early Twenties, but in Paddy's case I felt the discolouring was not due to excess sunshine.

"Well, be the look on your face, gasson, I hope that John Powers fella comes back to the Snug tonight and I'll tell ye if I can get that triduum of scholars enticed in the back dure, they'll not be getting home till they throw a bit of light on these shenanigans we're talking about."

Paddy was drumming the hazel rod off his "leggans", as he referred to the cut-off tops from the waterproof wellingtons he wore around his legs. They rested on his Shamrock brand leather boots – "keeps the legs of me corduroys clane, gasson, for Sunday," he explained. He began to recite once more:

> "Here comes the lad with the hazel
> And the folding star's in the rack
> 'Nights a good herd,' to the cattle,
> He sings, 'She brings all things back.'

# Militia Men

"Where was I, anyway?" Paddy asked. I said the schoolmasters were telling him about a bunch of vigilantes lying in Sleepy Hollow in New York state a couple of hundred years ago.

"They had a wee navey can of stur-a-bout with them that a dacent woman was after preparing for them. They were calling themselves militia men, but they were only slips of gassons at the time. The masters towel me the three militia men stopped a boyo on horseback. He wasn't sure whether the rider was headless or heedless and believe it or not the boyo they took off the horse was a British soldier and to bate the band the militia men found a bunch of private papers belonging to Washington on the Brit's person. Washington had left his papers in the charge of a skinflint named Arnold, and Arnold betrayed Washington by giving the papers to the Brit, whose name was André."

Paddy said the masters told him that those militia men changed the course of world history that day by apprehending Major André in Sleepy Hollow, where the militia men were on duty to stop the cattle rustlers from driving cattle to the British slaughter houses in New York; this was the morning of the 23rd September 1780.

"Then there was a professor some years back in Crosse doing a comparative study between Patrick Kavanagh and Henry David Thoreau who lived by himself in a cabin in the woods in a place called Walden Pond. Would that be anywhere near you back home, gasson?"

Paddy said he sat up at night trying to figure out the connection between another craic the masters read to him one night while he was fixing a goat's langle. He said the masters told him that George Washington – "the father of your great nation, gasson" – stopped at a house a couple of fields south from where the three vigilantes took the trousers off Major André.

"Paulding, Wart and Williams had another slip of a lad with them helping them loose the buckles off André's trousers. Washington made his ceilidh with an old friend, Jamsie Hammond, one night round about the same time on his way to a conference in Tarrytown in Westchester county. George and Jamsie were good friends from many years back. The night am telling you about was probably before the turn of the 19th century. Bear that in mind, me man.

"Didn't it bate the divil, gasson, that there was a British sympathizer watching Hammond's house to report to the Brits who might be going in or out? What did the boyo do but contact the British army and inform them about the Hammond's visitor, and the next thing Jamsie and his wife knew was the pounding on their dure, and before Jamsie could get his trousers on fully, the front dure was bruke down by the boots and guns of the Brits, and there was a heap of British soldiers with two cannons pointing at Jamsie demanding to know where Washington was."

Paddy continued, "That was then and this is now, and I can take you right now, gasson, a couple of fields south of Crossmaglen, up the Dundalk road, over across Sam's Lonin, across a few stone stiles, and I'll show you a front dure of a house the Brits bruck down with their boots and heavy guns in the Seventies. What do you make of it, gasson?

"Surely to God they couldn't be suspecting or thinking that the Hammonds might have relatives in Lissaraw from another life, and maybe the Brits believe the fairies in Lissaraw Fort brought Washington over for a night's craic. Ye think am codding ye, gasson, you can go out to Lissaraw and see the dure for yourself; it's there for the world to see. I'll tell ye more, you can have the lend of me ould girl's bike there and go out the Monog road and you will see plenty of dures where the Brits left their boot marks on.

"I was telling you there about the dacent woman who made the stur-a-bout for the militia men (there was seven of them) but they split that morn on the top of Kykuit Hill. She was on night duty in Sleepy Hollow, gasson. Her name was Frena and she was only a slip of a gersha when she left Switzerland and went to America. She married her childhood sweetheart and they had ten children and their neighbour was Jamsie Hammond. "Jamsie Hammond was in charge of purchasing pork for Washington's army."

Paddy was looking east from his observation 'throne of scone', as he sometimes referred to it ("but this one is in its right place, gasson; at least we didn't stale it from Scotland"). Just then I noticed a large, articulated truck with a trailer in tow parked on the top westerly end of the large square. It had multiple levels of floor decks which housed numerous live pork pigs.

"This one has me stumped, gasson. Frena's gasson was one of the seven militia men that helped change the course of world history that morn of September 23$^{rd}$, 1780, when they split on top of Kykuit Hill to stop the

British cattle rustlers from feeding British soldiers to reduce the Brits' ability to break down people's dures. Jamsie Hammond and Frena were feeding local gassons with fresh pork and stir-a-bout, and here we are looking at loads of fresh pork here in Crosse centuries later. What do you make of it all, gasson?

The Brits have moved their dure-brakin dissidents to Cross and all I know is the pork is still alive when it laves the Square. Do you have one of them con-cuter-mints" – by which he meant computers – "that could help you sort this whole mess out, gasson?"

Paddy teased out a well-earned pipeful of Carrol's No. 1. He cupped it in the heart of his hand while at the same time he imitated Tommy Makem with the rhythmic four-finger exercise around and upon his tobacco strings. Paddy then brought his left arm across to the right side of his body and commenced to employ his left index finger in between the cavities of his right fingers. Paddy was very frugal – or was it very artful? – in the tobacco teasing techniques; in fact, he was extremely artful in many, many teasing techniques. It was Swan match time again.

"The blessings of God on you, gasson, and may your hen always lay early in the morn."

Paddy hooked his left thumb behind his braces. It was recital time again.

> *"Ye grateful friends*
> *That hover round this stone*
> *And childer who in lacework gowns appear*
> *Tho' we're locked up from ye to Mills forelorn*
> *We must not shed our unavailable Teer*
>
> *Rejoice that tho' severe yer queenly doom*
> *Tho' cursed an strewn with roadblocks*
> *The pads we tread*
> *In Cross when unceasing*
> *Torture princely fed*
> *We'll howl our "Barrack Corner",*
> *Paddy said.*

Pat McEntegart

124

# Ireland, the First Colony

*No man is good enough to govern another man without that other's consent. When a man governs himself, that is self-government; but when he governs himself and also governs another man, then that is more than self-government – that is despotism. "Our reliance is in the love of liberty which God has planted in our bosoms, our defence is in the spirit which prizes liberty shall starve as the heritage of all men in all lands, everywhere. Those who deny freedom to others deserve it not for themselves, and under a just God cannot long retain it."*

On the second evening in which I visited Paddy, he immediately launched into his favourite subject, which is Britain's role in Irish affairs. He went to his kitchen table and retrieved some papers from the pull-out drawer which he said his schoolmaster friend took from the New York Public Library.

"Take a peep at them yourself, gasson," he said. "This problem with the Brits has been going on for over 1500 years."

Paddy said he had learned from his friend that independence from foreign rule was fuelled all over the world by the 1776 American war of independence.

"Remember what I towel yeh before about the definite decision in the minds and hearts of two men, Samuel Adams and John Hancock, in Boston on the night of March 5th, 1776. Note too that the great Irish parliamentarian Daniel O'Connell was just one year ould at this time in the history of Ireland."

The 1789 revolution of France and the liberating of some of the Mediterranean countries from Ottoman rule by the British, notably Greece in 1798, gave the Irish, again supported by the French, the encouragement to campaign for freedom from the British.

# Daniel O'Connell, the Father of Modern Irish Nationalism

The Irish had waited for someone to lead them out of hell for centuries, and finally, in 1775, the man was born. O'Connell was an early beneficiary of the Catholic Relief Act (1793), which permitted Catholics to be trained for the London Bar (Barristers of Advocates). Upon completing his training, O'Connell returned to Dublin to practice law. He dreamt of a peasant's revolution but one which avoided the bloodshed of the French version of which he had had direct experience during his school days in France.

# Victorian Times

The English were then the most powerful nation in the world but had no special place in their hearts for their oldest colony, Ireland, even though its inhabitants were white, mainly because they were Catholic and apparently economically without hope. While the Dickensian English Empire builders robbed the inhabitants of India and shot the aboriginal Australian natives plus 10 million North American buffalo for sport, they let a million Catholics in the potato-fed west of Ireland starve to death in the four years of the Great Hunger of 1845-49.

"They'll make restitution yet before I'm finished with them," Paddy said.

# Crossmaglen Conspiracy

Paddy said the so-called Crossmaglen Conspiracy of the 1880's rocked the Liberal government of the time brought the resignation of Joseph Chamberlain and O. J. Trevelyan and the return, following a general election, of a Tory Government.

It was nothing short of a government/landlord conspiracy to malign the whole district and its inhabitants, and it brought long imprisonment to twelve innocent men and death in prison to two and caused dozens to flee the country for fear of similar treatment. Most of them never returned. Lies were told, and false evidence concocted, particularly in a contrived document coded the "Crossmaglen Book of the Patriotic Brotherhood". The latter organization was never heard of, either before or since the trial.

The outrages that sparked the whole affair were said to be as follows:

A. On the 24th of January 1882, shots were fired over the house of the widow Kelly of Crievkeeran, who was rumoured, to be informing on her neighbours. Several eyewitness reports, that the two men who fired the shots returned immediately into the police barracks there, were ignored and suppressed.

B. A shop at Creggan was ransacked by unnamed individuals.

C. The two policemen implicated in the Widow Kelly attack went to the parish priest and asked him to speak out against "moonlighting" by secret societies among his congregation. He refused. Yet a special counsel sent by Dublin Castle to the Belfast trial later falsely testified that over and over again the clergyman of that neighbourhood warned his unfortunate flock to guard against the terrible gulf that was yawning before them when they entered secret societies. Henry Gustavus Brooke of the "Crossmaglen Clock" fomented the wild image of the district by making it known his life was under threat in South Armagh.

D. The bigoted Belfast Newsletter entered the fray with gusto, reproducing accounts of 30-year-old atrocities to illustrate Crossmaglen's reputed lawlessness. Under the Foster Coercion Act of 1881, five South Armagh men were arrested in Milltown House, Culloville. They were the balladeers Michael Watters and Denis Nugent, as well as James Hanratty of Creenkill, Patrick Finnegan of Lurgancullenboy and Thomas Kelly, all of the Land League, probably the real target.

E. Soon they were followed by four more from County Monaghan. Later five more were lifted, one of whom, Edward O'Hanlon of Mullaghbawn, was the first witness for the crown. He it was who testified that the Patriotic Brotherhood had been formed locally by Ribbonmen and other agrarian secret societies he named as the "Bogmen" and the "Rednecks". At the opening trial in Armagh, O'Hanlon retracted and admitted the whole thing was concocted. He was immediately charged as a co-conspirator. Another informer named Patrick Duffy, who lived at Culloville on the site of what is now Hoey's shop, was found and twelve of the thirteen defendants were found guilty. The thirteenth was living in Scotland at the time and couldn't possibly have been involved.

F. In all, 153 men were implicated in the forged document known as the "Crossmaglen Book of the Patriotic Brotherhood". It was never shown to the defence on the grounds that outstanding charges would later be levelled against the others – something, of course, that never happened. A further 65 men were named as co-conspirators in the parallel forged "Mullaghbawn Book". There was also a "Cullyhanna Book". In all, 300 tenant farmers were implicated.

G. The Crossmaglen Conspiracy became a cause in the House of Commons for Nationalist MPs Tim Healy and party leader Charles Steward Parnell. The last of the innocents were not released from prison until 1889. They had endured seven years of hard labour. Michael Watters died in prison.

H. Crossmaglen had acquired the loathsome image it has laboured under ever since.

# From Crossmaglen back to America

After I returned to the States from my trip to Crossmaglen in 1971 I spent a lot of my time digesting and simulating the knowledge I had received from Paddy. I kept thinking of his positive approach to his problems. His attitude had left an endearing stamp upon my personality. Surely there must be a way in which I could assist that much-disadvantaged community? Then again, I had to address my own problems and circumstances first. It was now 1976 and I was engaged in construction in New York. I was married with four young kids and two aged parents living close by. In my spare time I kept typing Paddy's story and continued to research ways and means of promoting peace in Crossmaglen.

As the years rolled by my health began to fail and my business began to tumble. With a young family and a heavy mortgage. I was in dire straits until eventually in 1978 I was hospitalized with a nervous breakdown. During my three-week stay in hospital, someone, I never found out who, gave me a copy of Norman Vincent Peale's book, *The Power of Positive Thinking*. I began reading it and repeating the Biblical affirmations within it together with the many formulas. I found it inspiring and I continued to repeat the affirmations as I strolled through the grounds of the hospital.

Then came the Saturday morn when I was being discharged. My doctor came in to me and sat on the corner of my bed. Knowing my situation at home and that things were bad, he said, "Mr Moore, what are you going to do about all your problems?"

I said, "Doctor, I don't know! All I know is I now have five young kids and a heavy mortgage, and two aged parents who are dependent on me, so I definitely cannot quit!"

The young Doctor stood up and said to me, "Aren't you the lucky man that cannot quit."

A short few days after my discharge from hospital I went to visit with my aunt Nan who lived a short distance from me at home, and call it woman's intuition if you will, but Nan obviously saw that all was not well with me. I wasn't my usual good self.

Nan left me sitting by her fireside in her sitting room and she went up into her bedroom. After about ten minutes or so she returned with a single page from a blue writing pad on which she had written, in her own handwriting, a poem which she handed to me saying, "That was our Patsy's prayer when he was dying of cancer."

I began to read it out loud.

> *When things go wrong as they sometimes will*
> *And the road you're trudging seems all uphill*
> *When the funds are low*
> *And the debts are high*
> *And you want to smile*
> *But you have to sigh*
> *When care is pressing you down a bit*
> *Rest if you must but don't you quit*
> *Life is queer with its twists and turns*
> *As every one of us sometimes learns*
> *And many a failure turns about*
> *When we might have won*
> *Had we stuck it out*
> *Don't give up though the pace seems slow*
> *You may succeed with another blow*
> *Success is failure turned inside out*
> *The silver tint on the clouds of doubt*
> *And you never can tell*
> *How close you are*
> *It may be near*
> *When it seems so far*
> *So stick to the fight*
> *When you're hardest hit*
> *It's when things seem worst*
> *That you must not quit.*

As I write these lines now, that was 40 years ago and that evening as I folded my poem into my wallet I thanked Nan several times because I then knew she had armed me with a weapon to overcome all of my problems. That was then and later I had my poem laminated to preserve it for all time and I have it on my desk in front of me all the time in memory of Nan Lennon, and if you are reading it for the first time please believe me it will get you through the tough days and nights. All I ask is that you remember Nan of 40 years ago.

And so I continued my studies and kept expanding my knowledge on the workings of the human mind. I read lots of material such as John Kehoe's *Mind Power* and Dr Joseph Murphy's *The Power of Your Subconscious Mind*. John Kehoe is a man who, like Henry David Thoreau, spent three years in the woods in intensive study and contemplation of the inner workings of the human mind. Dr Murphy has been acclaimed as a major figure in the human potential movement, the spiritual heir to writers like James Allen, Dale Carnegie, Napoleon Hill and Norman Vincent Peale.

Time swiftly passed, and my construction company was going strong in Manhattan. That was in the late Eighties. Then in 1990 I purchased a guesthouse and restaurant in Ireland. It had been advertised in the newspapers as fully licenced premises, so I stretched my resources and completed the sale and moved to Ireland and began to upgrade it.

When I had the premises ready for opening I invited the local fire officer out to check that everything was up to par. When he arrived and toured both the downstairs and upstairs he was shocked. He informed me that the bar and function rooms upstairs were illegal because there were no fire escapes. He further stated that his council had no record of the layout of these premises. He said I would have to engage an architect and submit drawings to obtain planning approval before he would allow me to open.

So there I was, with all my finances drained. In order to redeem the situation, I was forced to mortgage my ancestral property in Ireland which I had recently inherited from my father. Even so, the removal of all the violations cost me more than I realized so therefore I was unable to pay the monthly mortgage on the premises which I had structured with the previous owner. While I was rushing to complete the project, I was taken to the local court and was forced to hand back the keys of the premises. That was the 3$^{rd}$ of June 1991 I was broke – everything was lost – I was totally defeated.

As I left the courthouse I thought of Nan's poem: "It's when things seem worst you must not quit."

So I went home to Crossmaglen and moved into my ancestral home and right away I turned on the television in the corner of my living room, and right there on the screen was Liam Clancy of the world-famous, ballad-singing group "The Clancy Brothers and Tommy Makem". He approached the microphone and as he walked up he slung his guitar to the side like a Western gun slinger and he took a sip of water from a glass and began to speak. He said this song is about a ship that sank off the coast of Nova Scotia called "The Mary Ellen Carter"., He also said the song contained a wonderful last verse. Then he said he thought it was Bertal Wright, who said this:

"With a man's dying breath he should be prepared to make a fresh start."

Then Liam said, "This song is important because you may get some solace from it on occasions of sorrow." After that he began to sing. I was glued to my seat; it was incredible:

> *All ye to whom adversity had dealt its final blow*
> *With smiling bastards lying to ye everywhere you go*
> *Turn to, and put out all your strength of arm and heart and brain*
> *And like the Mary Ellen Carter "Rise again"*
> *Rise again; rise again, though your heart may be broken*
> *And life about to end*
> *No matter what you've lost, be it a home, a love, a friend,*
> *Like the Mary Ellen Carter, "Rise again".*

Liam Clancy that evening of 3$^{rd}$ June 1991 lifted me so high from my doldrums that I immediately jumped into my car and travelled to Crossmaglen, where I visited my cousin Peter Rogers and borrowed the price of my fare back to New York.

When I landed in NYC I took the subway to my son Adrian's apartment in Yonkers and borrowed his jeep and toured Manhattan until I found a construction site ready for building. Finally, after much effort, I spotted a plywood hoarding along Houston Street between Mott and Elizabeth Streets, so I parked and went in behind the fence which is now the site of the Soho Abbey building and spoke to the excavation contractor John Mulvihill, who gave me the number of the owner.

I then called the owner and set up an appointment to view the drawings of the project. When I visited the owner, I put him on notice that I was confident that I could complete his building at a reasonable cost and within his timeframe. After a couple of meetings we agreed on my price, but he said he would require a guarantor. So I called my good friend John Keown of the Ballyfree Foundation, who had a large portfolio of real-estate in Queens and who willingly signed as guarantor for me to complete the project. God bless John; only for him I would never have gotten the job. I then had the contract, but there was a snag: I had no money, though I did have good credit in New York. So I structured the contract with a clause in it which would guarantee me a payment of $10,000 at the end of the first week on the job. I then asked the work crew to work a lying week, which they agreed to do – so at the end of the second week when the cheque had cleared the bank I would be able to pay the work crew. But still I had another pressing problem: I had to eat for that week.

So I walked around the block from the jobsite until I came to Bella's café on the corner of Elizabeth Street and spoke with Bella herself. I told her I was doing the construction job up the street and she agreed to give me credit for a week's worth of food. My three sons worked together on the project for no pay to recover our ancestral home in Ireland. Michael, my eldest, was in charge of the work crews; Adrian was overseeing the bricklayers and supervising the weekly crane delivery of the steel flooring, while Patrick, the youngest at 16 years, was working as a carpenter laying the floor decking.

I received partial payments as each floor was finished right up to the roof at the tenth floor, and with the profits from this project I was able to clear the debts off my property in Ireland.

By now it was close to 1993 and work in construction had slowed down. I was out of debt but I was also out of a job, and stone broke because a cheque which I had received from work performed at Newark Airport NJ had bounced. Now living in a one-bedroom apartment on Steinway Street in Queens, I was unable to pay my rent. Things again had turned bleak for me. My landlord had turned off the water supply to my apartment. I was living on coffee and bran muffins daily. I was forced to collect soda cans.

The money I earned from this venture went to purchase subway tokens which brought me to my son Adrian in Yonkers, with him I had earlier arranged that he would leave an odd twenty-dollar bill for me occasionally in the ashtray of an old car I had abandoned outside of his apartment. Through it all, I kept saying to myself "This Too Shall Pass" and "God's Delays Are Not God's Denials" and I just kept on reading and studying and writing and praying.

Very soon it was the turn of my good friend John Keown who once again came to my rescue by offering me a free apartment in the Hart Building at William Street in Ossining, New York, where I got some masonary work from homeowners .In between work spells, a very kind blind neighbour lady gave me some tinned foods as she sensed my circumstances were not great at that time. Harriet Miller is her name.

After I had been a long period in the Hart Building, John Keown offered me the management of an antique store at 25 Main Street, Tarrytown. This was a large store with 20 dealers in it; I moved into an apartment on the second floor and installed a female manager in the store to allow me to continue with my construction work. Then in 1998 I registered a 501(3)(c), not-for-profit charitable corporation in New York with the right to work with NGO's in Ireland. However, in 2000 my health failed severely and the doctors in Westchester County Hospital advised me to relocate to Ireland.

Nothing happens except first a dream the belief hat becomes truth for me is that which allows me the best use of my strenght; the best means of putting my vertues into action——Aundra Geld

# Paddy's Dream

Soon after I left Paddy, he had a telephone installed, so that I could keep in touch with events in Crossmaglen. Some years after that came the Good Friday Agreement and things became more peaceful. New businesses began opening in the town and shoppers came from far and near. Paddy adopted new voluntary measures to improve the wellbeing of his neighbours. He dreamed of one day of having a charity to help those in need physically and mentally, and he shared his vision with me over the phone.

During one of these conversations in the late 1990's, Paddy, a humble man of simple means,told me he had a dream one night in the late 1990's. His dream was in the form of a vision of a "House of Peace for Crossmaglen". At that time, Paddy, who was living in a one-bedroom cottage in Crossmaglen, was engaged in the construction of a two-storey dwelling. The next morning after his dream, Paddy pondered over breakfast how the vision had come to him during sleep. The building had appeared as if above a misty valley, triangular in shape with three equal sloping walls of 60 degrees. The side walls sloping, such were made of sufficient straw bales and would be left vacant up the roof and the various floors acted as support beams for the roof. The floor beams, which were made up of concrete bison slabs, were each laid out over the triangular areas in the shape of a Celtic cross.

The load-bearing centre walls were constructed of 48-inch round bales of straw, all of which was enclosed in 48-inch tubular steel scaffolding. The entry points for pedestrian traffic to the various floors would be via the 48-inch steel scaffolding, and sufficient straw bales would be left vacant to provide for running the elevators at key locations. Fire-proofing to all walls would be performed by draped-on mesh or jute covers together with spray-on coating.In Paddy's dream there was room for a small hotel within the ground floor. Building areas would be allocated to conference rooms and assembly would be laid out on the ground floor with offices prepared for the Cultural Revival of South Armagh and beyond. ("Help shall gather," Paddy prayed.)

Wooh! What a dream! – I had known from spending time with Paddy that he possessed "creative imagination", and judging from his behaviour I assumed he also employed his "sixth sense" and from time to time I had reason to believe that he had an abundance of clairvoyance into the bargain.

I also knew that Paddy was very close to nature and that he cared deeply about the environment because he had talked to me about the power of the sun and wind as well as the heat from the Earth's surface. So it was no great surprise to me when he told me he was thinking of a solar system for his dream "House of Peace". He said he lay awake at night thinking about ways of harnessing the solar energies, and he went further by saying he was planning a system of drying the wet sludge waste from his house and using it as fuel to heat the home. I was nearly speechless with amazement, but I motivated him by saying, "What the mind of man can conceive and believe, the mind of man can achieve." I knew that Paddy was sharp, that he possessed a brilliant mind, he had quick thinking and he would never shy away from a challenge, so I told him I would help him fulfil his dream.

Time moved on. It was the Nineties then and Paddy was moving his idea along. He told me he had been sketching some concepts on paper. "I can't write, but I can draw," he told me over the phone. I told him to take his drawings to a printer in Newry and have him convert them into PDF files and have the print shop e-mail them to me in New York. I had earlier sent my email address to Paddy by post so he could take it to the print shop. He did all that and when I received his sketches I was very impressed because they contained very accurate details. So I mailed him a signed non-competing, non-disclosure agreement and told him to take it to his solicitor in town to make sure his idea was safe.

Sometime after that I decided that I would take another trip to Crossmaglen. I was anxious to move Paddy's dream ahead, so when I arrived in Crossmaglen I was pleasantly surprised at how things had changed for the better over the decades. Business was booming, there was a new hotel with 15 bedrooms, new shops, and the Square was lined with expensive-looking cars and trucks. The people on the streets were happy and friendly, children played happily in the adjoining parks without disruption, and there was an air of prosperity all around.

After my visit with Paddy, who looked extremely well, I contacted a local architect and an electrical/mechanical consultant and together we set up a mastermind alliance group to brainstorm Paddy's idea. I then contacted a company in the UK and engaged them to conduct a patent search with the view to applying for a worldwide patent.

Again the years rolled on quickly. I had some health problems and things were put on the back burner for some time, but Paddy kept on revising his plans. On some occasions when we spoke on the phone he would be a little despondent, saying things like, "I have a long ways to go." But my sole aim was to keep him motivated during the trying times. So I would say to him:

"Do not be discouraged by the distance you still have to travel; instead, appreciate the many life-miles you have already covered, y. Your struggle has made you a stronger and better person; do not let anyone dissuade you from blooming into the person you are meant to be. Keep walking!"

I also advised him to keep his plans to himself, not to discuss them with anyone because they would think he was crazy. Remember what happened to the Wright Brothers when they announced they had invented a machine that could fly: Their family had them locked in a mental institution! So I advised Paddy to keep his thoughts and plans to himself. I said, "Tell the world what you're going to do, but show them first!" Paddy liked that.

After that I contacted a body to prepare a business plan for the project, and then made an application to Invest Northern Ireland for seed money to pay the professionals involved and to purchase a suitable site. Later on, I heard again from the engineers in the UK and got further feedback. Their comments were very encouraging:

> *We really believe that the concept has potential and would like to offer our help in developing this. The first step we recommend is to turn your concept into a three-dimensional Computer Aided Design (3D CAD) model. With this stage complete we will show you how to apply for intellectual property (IP) protection on the concept before you disclose it to anybody. Either way, we believe it is only worth reviewing the intellectual property of your concept after this visualisation stage.*

During further visits to Paddy's cottage, it became clear to me that he had a true vision of what should happen for the people of Crossmaglen. He said they had been deprived for centuries and this was the cause for so much unrest. Paddy confessed to me that he would like to see Crossmaglen brought more in line with the surrounding towns of Newry, Dundalk, Castleblaney and Carrickmacross, where there were modern facilities like swimming pools, saunas, spas and golf courses. He went on to elaborate his vision which extended to a Community Peace Centre with residential accommodation for retired citizens as well as healthcare facilities and places for children and adults with special needs.

Paddy was so serious about his dream for Crossmaglen, that he convinced me that the money to build his dream would turn up at the appropriate time. Because Crossmaglen is a disadvantaged area, he insisted that funding would become available in the interests of a true and lasting peace initiative which would integrate Crossmaglen with the rest of the world.

Once again Paddy had left me with much to ponder. I decided to meet with my architect to put forward Paddy's proposal for what he termed the "Global House of Peace" for Crossmaglen using his previous concept of the triangular building from his dream. Then I waited the outcome.

Something else was emerging from my frequent visits to Paddy. I noticed that there was in Paddy's tone and speech a deep spirituality; he believed he was divinely guided.

# Paddy's Vision

Expanding further on his vision for Crossmaglen, Paddy said he believed in the people of Cross, who in former years had built churches, schools, sports facilities etc., and he truly believed the present generation would do it again. They are brilliant technicians, skilled crafts persons, entrepreneurs, medical experts, engineers etc., and "they can do anything they put their minds to. Paddy said that we do not have to bring violence into our lives; there is another way, yet we will not find that way by searching for it, we will only find it by creating it, and we will not create it by being stuck in old beliefs, but only by opening ourselves to new ideas. New ideas about God and about life can truly light our world. Paddy said, that life is a process of awakening, and he suggested that we form a team in Crossmaglen called the "Humanities Team" to do this work.

The time of the single master is over; it is now time to work together in multiple numbers. We can ask people everywhere to work together to create a space of possibility for a new spirituality to emerge upon our community; everyone has the ability to convey this message of at oneness. You have all the gifts of communication that you ever require; your message is your life lived, your gift is your divine self-expressed talent; simply allow yourself to be expressed in your own unique way. Others see their possibility in the reality of you; be therefore a model for all the world, be the hope of humanity, trust the love that flows through you, trust the truth that lives within you, trust the process of life itself, that is you. It will bring you to the exact way, the perfect conditions, and just the right moments to allow you to become the message you wish to send. Trust in this process and you will have this experience. It's important only to be responsible for yourself. You do your part, don't worry about the person next to you, otherwise if you're not careful you'll be waiting for the person next to you and they'll be waiting for the person next to them and so on and nothing will ever happen, nothing will ever get started.

So start with the tools you have and better tools will be given to you as you go along. Remember that you don't get what you want, you get what you expect.

Paddy straightened himself up after all that and asked me to relay his wishes to the people of Crossmaglen and beyond. Slowly it became clearer to me that Paddy was always employing "possibility thinking"; his peaceful mind generates creative ideas which produce enthusiasm which is energy! So his possibility-thinking, peace-centred mind is constantly and enthusiastically planning, creating and producing ideas which stimulate boundless energy to achieve incredible goals.

"I believe God gives me power to attain what I really want," he then said. "I expect the best and with God's help will attain the best!"

On another visit to Paddy, I found him engaged in having his boundary drain cleaned by a mechanical excavator in his garden. Over coffee he said he was studying the workings of the machine and its hydraulic system. In particular he said he paid a lot of attention to the mechanics of the stationary jacks and the tilting action of the front-loading shovel. It was then he said he decided to employ hydraulics into the operating of his design for his sludge waste system. This got me thinking, so when I returned home I set up a meeting to discuss Paddy's drawings. Paddy had said that he envisioned raising the wet sludge up from the tank bottom to the dryer then onto a conveyor to a hopper above a pellet machine where the pellets could be bagged.

During a further visit Paddy expanded on his vision for the Community Peace Centre. He maintained that Crossmaglen should have its own swimming pool/sauna and spa.

"Why not?" he said. "Shure, people would come from near and far to partake in the activities, especially when there was also an ice-rink and gymnasium and a tennis and squash court into the bargain. Why not?"

He also suggested a small boxing arena for the youths of the area.

"What you need to do, avick," he said, "is to begin to visualize the buildings in your mind. Before an architect designs a building he first creates an image of the concept in his mind. Before he puts pen to paper, he imagines. That's what the ancients done in the underground caves in France, gasson, they chiselled out carvings of pregnant sheep and goats and llamas. They were projecting prosperity in the coming season.

"You need to start visualizing the finished project in your mind's eye, avick," he continued. "That's what I did before I sketched my designs, ah made a mental picture in my mind. You should also begin to imagine large sums of money coming into your bank account to build this project. Remember the money is out there somewhere; you need to create a vehicle to bring it in like a magnet. Act as though you are and you will be!"

As I crossed the Cappy fields back home to Lissaraw street, after my visit, I pondered deeply on Paddy's words of wisdom – create a vehicle, he had said. It was then I realized I already had that vehicle in the form of the local charity. Somehow I would begin to solicit donations and funding from various sources globally. Paddy had planted a certified seed in my fertile mind and there it would germinate.

# The Victory of Faith

On another occasion when I visited Paddy I found him bent over his fire, placing an antique soldering iron into the flames. He stood up and greeted me then began pouring over his kitchen table, deeply engrossed in the ancient art of Celtic stained-glass creation. He was putting together the Celtic Love Knot which he said was the symbol of the Holy Trinity, though to Paddy it also symbolized the three religions of Ireland.

What impressed me most about Paddy was his ability to carry on, even in the face of severe adversity. I asked him what motivated him to keep going after every setback.

"Lying down during a time of grief," he responded, "or being quiet after a financial setback, certainly implies great strength, but I know of something that suggests even greater strength – the power to continue working after a setback, the power to still run with a heavy heart, and the power to perform your daily tasks with deep sorrow in your spirit. This is a Christ-like thing!

"It is in these places of severe testing, with no human way out of our difficulty, that our faith grows and is strengthened!"

Paddy continued, "The path of faith is one of sorrow and joy, suffering and healing comfort, tears and smiles, trials and victories, conflicts and triumphs, and also hardships, dangers, beatings, persecutions, misunderstandings, trouble and distress," he said. "Yet in all things we are more than conquerors through him who loved us." (Romans 8:37).

Then he said that true sympathy comes from understanding another person's hurt by suffering the same affliction. Therefore we cannot help others who suffer without paying a price ourselves, because afflictions are the cost we pay for our ability to sympathize. Those who wish to help others must first suffer. If we wish to rescue others, we must be willing to face the cross.

"God is going to test you with delays, Paddy told me, "and along with the delays will come suffering." Yet through it all, he said, God's promise stands. I have his new covenant in Christ, and His sacred promise of every smaller blessing that I need. The delays and the suffering are actually part of the promised blessings, so I should praise Him for them today. May I "be strong and take heart and wait on the Lord" (Psalm 27:14).

Our training for a life of faith requires many areas of learning, Paddy said, including the trial of faith, the discipline of faith, the patience of faith and the courage of faith. Often, he said, we will pass through many stages before we finally realize the result of faith – namely, the victory of faith.

It is commonly thought that a protected and easy life is the best way to live. Yet, as Paddy observed, the lives of all the noblest and strongest people prove exactly the opposite and the endurance of hardship is the making of the person. It is the factor that distinguishes between merely existing and living a vigorous life. Hardship builds character.

But what shall I do? He said, "I expect to pass through this world but once. Therefore, any good work, kindness or service I can render to any person or animal, let me not neglect or delay to do it, for I will not pass this way again."

I noticed on his table he had a pyramid-shaped Celtic lampshade. He said it represented the three governments involved in the Good Friday Agreement as well as Protestant, Catholic and Dissenter in Ireland and beyond.

"I was towel by my grandfather that life should always be based on forgiving your neighbour. When Saint Peter asked our Lord, Would seven times be enough to forgive one who had wronged you? our Lord replied No, but seven times seventy!"

That was the number of pieces Paddy had put in place to make up his lamp of forgiveness.

"One hundred and sixty-three pieces on each side equals 489 and the light bulb makes it 490," Paddy said, and then he asked me to try and get someone to make it commercially for sale for the local charity.

# The Great Hunger

I visited Paddy later that week, and over coffee he began a discussion on the major dependence England had in former years on Irish food products. He said he had it from his schoolmaster friend who had researched it in a New York Public Library that an incident had occurred some centuries ago in which French pirates seized 200 firkins of Irish butter en route to the London market off the south coast of Ireland, which caused the price on the London market to rise by 100%. Paddy also then told me he had compiled detailed lists of the boat loads of food which was shipped from Ireland at the point of bayonets during An Gort Na Mor, the Great Hunger.

At this point he slid open the top drawer of his nearby dresser and extracted some papers, one of which was an ancient map of Ireland which clearly showed the Genocide of the British regiments and the ships that removed the food between 1845 and 1848 from the starving Irish. I was stunned,

"Everyone knows the potato failed," Paddy said, "but there was beef, pork, fish, corn, barley, wheat, milk, butter, cheese, vegetables!" What's more, he said, the Irish fishermen were bound under a 1770 English law to smear their nets with tar and oil which prevented the fish from entering their nets, while the English fishermen were encouraged to smear their nets with oak bark that attracted the fish.

I began reading the reports that Paddy had collected which stated that the Public Records Office informed persons that their British regiment's daily activity reports of 1845-1850 had "gone missing". Those records included the cattle drives and grain-cart convoys each regiment escorted at gunpoint from the Irish districts assigned to it. Also "missing" were the receipts issued by the British Army commissariat officers in every port tallying the cattle and tonnage of foodstuff removed, likewise the export lading manifests.

# The Food Removal

From Cork harbour on one day in 1847, the Ajax steamed for England with 1,514 firkins of butter, 102 casks of pork, 44 hogsheads of whiskey, 844 sacks of oats, 247 sacks of wheat, 106 bales of bacon, 13 casks of ham, 145 casks of porter, 12 sacks of fodder, 28 bales of feathers, 8 sacks of lard, 296 boxes of eggs, 30 head of cattle, 90 pigs, 220 lambs, 34 calves and 69 miscellaneous packages.

On November 14th, 1848, three ships sailed from Cork alone: 147 bales of bacon, 120 casks and 135 barrels of pork, 5 casks of hams, 149 casks of miscellaneous foodstuffs, 1,996 sacks and 950 barrels of oats, 300 bags of flour, 300 head of cattle, 239 sheep, 9,398 firkins of butter and 542 boxes of eggs.

The record for July 28th, 1848 details a typical day of food shipments from just four ports:

From Limerick, the ANN, the JOHN GUISE and the MESSENGER for London; the PELTON CLINTON for Liverpool; and the CITY OF LIMERICK, the BRITISH QUEEN, and the CAMBRIAN MAID for Glasgow. This one-day removal of Limerick's food comprised 863 firkins of butter, 212 firkins of cheese, 1,198 casks and 200 kegs of lard, 87 casks of ham, 267 bales of bacon, 52 barrels of pork, 45 tons and 628 barrels of flour, 4,975 barrels of oats and 1000 barrels of barley.

From Kilrush, the ELLEN for Bristol and the CHARLES G FRYER and the MARY ELLIOT for London. This one-day removal was of 550 tons of County Clare's oats and 15 tons of barley.

From Tralee, the JOHN ST BARBE, CLAUDIA and QUEEN for London; the SPOKESMAN for Liverpool. This one-day removal comprised 711 tons of Kerry's oats and 118 tons of barley.

From Galway, the MARY, the VICTORIA, and the DILIGENCE for London; the SWAN and the UNION for Limerick (probably transhipped to England). This one-day removal comprised 60 sacks of Galway flour, 30 sacks and 292 tons of its oatmeal, 294 tons of its oats and 140 tons of miscellaneous food stuff. British soldiers forcibly removed it from its starving producers in Limerick, Clare, Kerry and Galway.

In Belmullet, County Mayo, the mission of 151 soldiers of the 49th regiment was to guard a few tons of meal from the hands of the starving; its population fell from 237 to 105 between 1841 and 1851. Belmullet also lost its source of fish in January 1849, when British coast guards arrested its fleet of fishermen ten miles at sea in the act of off-loading flour from a passing ship. They were sentenced to prison and their currachs were confiscated.

In another paper I read the following:

The Waterford Harbour British Army commissariat officer wrote to British Treasury Chief Charles Trevelyan on April 24th, 1846: "The barges leave Clonmel once a week for this place, with export supplies under convoy which last Tuesday consisted of 2 guns, 50 cavalry and 80 infantry escorting them on the banks of the SUIR as far as Carrick." While its people starved, the Clonmel district exported annually, along with its other farm produce, approximately 60,000 pigs in the form of cured pork.

This to me was very shocking – then they'll ask what is the problem the Irish have with England? Paddy said over coffee – Ireland starved because its food, from 40 to 70 shiploads per day was removed at gunpoint by 12,000 British constables reinforced by the British militia, battleships, excise vessels, Coast Guards and by 200,000 British soldiers (100,000 at any given moment). .

In this way Britain seized from Ireland's producers tens of millions of head of livestock and tens of millions of tons of flour, grains, meat, poultry and dairy products, enough to sustain 18 million people.

Paddy said he had authentic evidence that almost 4,000 British ships were employed during the year 1847 to carry food from Ireland to the major ports of Liverpool, London, Bristol and Glasgow. Over half of them went to Liverpool, where many Irish ran out of money as they strove to make their way across the Atlantic.

Records show that ports in some of the worst-affected parts of Ireland, including Kilrush, Westport, Limerick, Ballyshannon, Bantry, Sligo and Ballina, where thousands upon thousands were dying of starvation, were also sending food to the mainland.

Paddy stated that historians now agree that British Government policies deliberately led to the deaths of hundreds of thousands of Irish people, leading many to proclaim that there never was a Great Famine.

# Awful Conditions and Prospects in County Mayo

This state of things shall not, however, prevent my once more soliciting public attention to the condition and prospects of that most afflicted portion of my country, my native county of Mayo. I shall confine my course as much as possible to a faithful, unvarnished statement of facts, for which I most urgently implore consideration.

On the 17th of August 1846, Lord John Russell spoke, in Parliament, as follows:

> *The whole credit of the Treasury and means of the country are ready to be used, as it is our bounden duty to use them, and will, whenever they can be applied, be so disposed as to avert famine, and to maintain the people of Ireland.*

On the 25th of the same month, Mr Labouchere, then a colleague of the noble Lord, spoke, also in Parliament, as follows;

> *He admitted that Mayo was one of the most distressed parts of the country, and one upon which the calamity had fallen with greater severity than upon others. I feel certain that the reduction of the population of Mayo, since 1846, is moderately estimated at 100,000 persons of all ages. On an average, I should calculate that the deaths, by famine, constitute at least one half of the diminution, and certainly the rapid extension of several burial places tends to confirm this impression.*

No. 1

From a reverend parish priest (April 7th):

"I have with grief to tell you, that at no period within the recollection of the oldest man living, has destitution been more general, nor one-twentieth so destructive in its murderous results. If ever the humane made exertions in favour of a perishing nation, Ireland, and particularly Mayo, commands that sympathy at this dread moment of her calamity."

No. 3

From a reverend parish priest, April 9th"It is very difficult indeed to convey to you any idea of the privations of the poor of this district. To form the correct estimate, you should witness daily and hourly the squalid misery and wasted forms of our starving and half-naked poor, who with sepulchral wail call for relief. The recipients of out-door relief are obliged to spend the greater portion of the day breaking stones, which system answers no purpose except to demonstrate the folly of the individuals who suggested, and continue still to enforce, a test which paralyses industry and prevents the poor from making a provision for the future. The wretched pittance of 1 lb. of Indian meal doled out to them in lieu of labour, is insufficient to support them, considering the trying circumstances in which they are placed, without houses or clothing to shelter them from the inclemency of the weather. To these unparalleled hardships I am induced to attribute the frightful ravages which fever and dysentery are at present committing among them. The greater part of the land is thrown out of cultivation, for the poor, who are still clinging to their tenements, have neither money nor seed to raise a crop for the ensuing season; and the small farmers, panic-struck by the visitation of the past and still darker prospects of the future, are repairing to some more favoured country, with the view of bettering their condition. Labour, the poor man's capital, is at present a regular drug in the market. The highest sum given is three pence a day, and many offer their labour for diet.

No. 10

From a reverend parish priest, April 12th"I take leave to state, that the condition of the poor in Crossmolina is miserable to the extreme. This parish contains 73,000 acres, the greater portion reclaimable bog. In 1841 its population exceeded 12,000 souls; at present, about 6,000. In March 1884, 5,300 were receiving relief; in March 1849, 3,300. If then the present system of what is called relief be continued one year longer, the entire pauper population must be got rid of. No other result could be expected. Firstly, not an individual was put on the relief list until he was reduced to a skeleton; his appearance was made the test of his distress. Such a one might linger for a few months; he would not recover. Secondly half a pound of meal is the average daily allowance, and this, in many instances the worst possible description. Thus in this parish, 3,300 having relief, having dependant on them 1,000 more; all not parents being disqualified. The quantity of meal weekly distributed, seven tons – 15,680 lbs. – which gives 3.5 lbs per person. Those who were able-bodied were obliged to work 10 hours per day."

Paddy then retrieved more documents from the second drawer of his kitchen table which highlighted the plight of the famine children who were separated from their parents by the British and suffered greatly.

During the famine parents entering workhouses were forced to separate from any children they had over two years of age. It had to have been an agonizing choice: Keep your family together and starve or save yourself but likely never see your kids again as they were transported to children's workhouses, often far away.

Bio-archaeologist Dr Jonny Geber, from UCC, who examined the skeletons of over 500 children unearthed from a mass grave in Kilkenny said the evidence shows they suffered greatly before they died. He said the stress on children who were removed from their parents caused massive problems.

It is really sad to think about the youngest children trying to cope with this situation and how many of them ended up dying in the workhouse.

"With this research, I can tell the story of those who did not survive the famine, which is a story that has never been told. Through interpreting their skeletons, you can get a unique insight. It would have been a severely traumatic experience to have entered the workhouse, especially for children, as they would have lost their parents through segregation if they weren't already orphans," said Dr Geber.

There were 545 children in total, but of these, two-thirds were less than six years of age, yet the workhouse recorded that the mortality rate of infants under the age of two was four times higher than for these older children

Even though the famine was already brutal enough with the prevalence of malnutrition and highly contagious diseases, these children were subjected to an extra layer of suffering through the intense distress they were caused by intensive work and separation from their parents.

At this point I could see that Paddy was profoundly affected by these events and he went on to say that he was expected to accept a lame apology from Tony Blair, who admitted the rulers in London at the time of the "Great Hunger" in Ireland had failed the people.

"An admission is one thing, gasson," Paddy said, "but they have yet to make full restitution to the Irish nation. It amazes me when I think of it how it is that people don't examine England's record worldwide over the centuries. Take your own country, America, avick: it was under British rule for years until one famous day a decision was made to end it.

Napolean Hill in his book "Think and Grow Rich" gave a detailed account of the launching of the war of independence as follows.

That day, which Paddy described as the most important date in American history, has been completely missed by historians and writers and reporters, he said. It was the 5th of March 1770, and on that day British soldiers were openly parading the streets of Boston provoking the residents into conflict. They then shot dead several civilians, most of whom had Irish sounding names: Patrick Carr, Samuel Gray, Samuel Maverick James Caldwell and an African Crispus Attucks. Three others were injured. That evening two men sat down and made a definite positive decision, which was to oust all British soldiers from Boston.

"Remember that a definite decision in the minds of two men is what brought about the freedom you now enjoy in the United States," Paddy told me. "Those two men were Samuel Adams and John Hancock, and from their decision that day came about the Correspondence committee and then came the Declaration of Independence, but without the first definite decision there could never have been a fight for freedom."

Over a second coffee, Paddy asked me to draw a parallel between that fatal day in Boston and August 15th, 1971, in Belfast when British soldiers shot dead Harry Thornton, an innocent Crossmaglen father of three on his way to work.

"Around the same time British cabinet minister Merlyn Rees – or was it Willie Whitelaw? – declared war on Crossmaglen, so we had no choice but to fight back," Paddy said.

That night there was rioting in Crossmaglen and a meeting was conducted in a cottage on the border known locally as the "TEER" border where a decision was reached to remove the Brits from Crossmaglen.

Paddy said that whenever the rebellion began in the United States, the British governor of Massachusetts, Governor Gage, sent Colonel Felton to Samuel Adams with a message which stated that Adams was to cease immediately from all hostilities against the Crown and to make his peace with the king, for which he would be greatly enumered (bribes), or else face deportation to England, where he would be hanged for high treason.

"You could say Adams was on the spot," Paddy said. "Adams asked for and got Colonel Felton's word of honour that he would repeat his reply to the Governor exactly as he —said it: 'Then you may tell Governor Gage that I have long since made my peace with the King of Kings and no amount of inducement will cause me to turn my back on my people. And you may tell Governor Gage that it is the advice of Samuel Adams to cease insulting the feelings of an exasperated people.'"

The rest is history.

Now to go back to Paddy's designs for the sludge waste recycling system, in February 2018 I met with, a mechanical engineer James,who agreed to mentor me in a new concept which involved a cylindrical in-ground tank with a top dome that will house the methane gas from the sewer. James also suggested a bucket elevator system to bring the sludge to the ground level.

By now it was February 26th, 2018. By this time Paddy, because of increasing years and because he needed to avail of "the mod cons", as he put it, decided to vacate his lone cottage and move into a converted, two-storey barn which had been modernized to suit his needs in Lissaraw Street, Crossmaglen, next door to me. It was there I found him demonstrating the use of the ancient Gaelic "lai", meaning spade, now called the loy spade, which was in use in Ireland prior to the "Great Hunger".

Back in December 2017, Paddy had purchased for himself a small car to "get around the neighbours" and to contact his associates in local towns. This was a major boost for him, he said: "It gives me more scope to fulfil my goals."

On another visit to Paddy, I found him engrossed in the topic of life's struggles. He said that through all his adversities, trials and setbacks he always referred back.

# Crossmaglen Again

So now in 2014 I was back in the vicinity of Crossmaglen again, continuing to move Paddy's design on still further and for the past 16 years I have discussed with Paddy and the professionals involved, the final approach to bring all this to fruition.

Then, on September 9th, 2015, severe tragedy struck me once again. This time it was the death of my beloved son Adrian from cancer at the young age of 44 years. A brilliant craftsperson and astute mind, I miss him dearly, but I truly believe he is guiding my every move from above. After that I scheduled a meeting with the engineers for the first week of October 2017 in Salisbury. Meantime I was keeping in close contact with Paddy in his cottage which is only across the fields, a short distance from me in the adjoining townland of Cappy. It wasn't unusual to find him in his garden each time I visited him, and more times I found him whitewashing the cottage or cleaning out his spring well.

After my visit, I returned via the Cappy mass pad (path) to Lissaraw and found myself reflecting upon my experiences with Paddy. I used the Welsh term *gwers*, which is Welsh for lessons. The word *gwers* is similar to *gweres*, meaning "a ray of sunshine". As it happened each visit to Paddy became a ray of sunshine, warming, enlightening and vitalising. Every visit began with a seed idea, in the form of thought or quotation. These ideas I would use as a prompt for meditation during the coming weeks and I found that the ideas spoke to me. Sometimes I even found it useful to write them down on a card which I would leave by the bed or in the kitchen. Even if I did not consciously read it often, my brain would register its message many times through the process of subliminal perception, and in that way my thoughts would act as a positive subconscious influence. I am amazed when I realize that this newfound discovery is all coming from Paddy, so I continued to ponder upon this.

It began to become clear to me from my conversations with him that in his own way Paddy was trying to teach me a connection with the earth, the sky, the moon, the stars, the four elements, the seasons, animals, stones and plants, and trees in particular. Paddy said being connected to these means we are actively communing. And Paddy was also trying to teach me a way of communing with Nature and with the divine spiritual source that manifests through the natural world.

Paddy taught me a way of looking at the world which emphasises the sacredness of all life, and our part in the web of creation. Over the years I discovered that Paddy cares deeply about the preservation and protection of the environment and that his approach is pragmatic, idealistic, spiritual and romantic.

On another occasion Paddy tried putting me in touch with Nature. He had a set of practices that helped me feel at one again with Nature, with my ancestors, my own body, my sense of Spirit, by thinking in specific ways about plants, trees, stones, animals and ancestral stories.

Paddy also had another practise that promoted healing and rejuvenation using spiritual and physical methods in a way that promotes health and longevity.

# The Dream Unfolding

Following that, I visited Paddy again and found him deeply engrossed with sorting out some acorns on his table. He proceeded to deposit them into a pail of water and watch for some of them to float to the surface.

"Those are not good for planting," he said.

He took the good ones and put them in a bag. At the same time I noticed a battery core drill with an auger placed on his chair close by. He then described to me the origins of the ancient wood of "Dunreavy" in South Armagh.

He said that in the 1500's, Dunreavy wood stretched from the Fane River east of Crossmaglen all the way right across South Armagh to the Clanyre River in Newry and that it straddled the Armagh/Louth border into the townland of Edenkill in County Louth. It was stated at the time that the trees were so dense that a squirrel could hop from one tree to the other without touching the ground.

Paddy said that in 1603, Henry II ordered the trees to be cut down because he believed they were hiding the bandits, so that's where the term bandit comes from. Paddy said he was anxious to launch a tree-planting project to refurbish what he called "Dunreavy-once-more". His plan was to start at the site of the peace centre and work out with the permission of the land owners throughout South Armagh. He said he had a friend who could organize software for plotting the course of the tree planting so people donating could visit their own personally labelled tree in the various seasons. He then broke into verse once again:

# Dunreavy-Once-More

The cutting of the trees
Had caused grave indignation
Cause 'tis written
That their leaves
Are for the healing
Of the nations
Rise up, Dunreavy
Rise up, become a book
Rise up their axe
Is consummated
In your brook
Sit I on porch unshaded
While Dunreavy sleeps her sleep
How long, how long, how long?
My Cross and "The Fews" must weep
But wait – a gain – a new dawn
Dunreavy in the lawn
White dove of peace
On tender limb I see
In my island forest
The lion protects the fawn

# Paddy's Life lessons

Paddy said he wanted to leave the readers with some lessons he had learned from his 90-year-old neighbour friend. Feel free to spread them around with friends and family:

- Life isn't fair, but it's still good.
- When in doubt, just take the next small step.
- Life is too short not to enjoy it.

# Your job won't take care of you when you are sick, your friends and family will.

- Don't buy stuff you don't need.
- You don't have to win every argument. Stay true to yourself.
- Cry with someone; it's more healing than crying alone.
- It's okay to get angry with God, he can take it.
- Save for things that matter.
- When it comes to chocolate, resistance is futile.
- Make peace with your past so it won't screw up your present.
- It's okay to let your children see you cry.
- Don't compare your life to others; you have no idea what their journey is all about.
- If a relationship has to be secret, you shouldn't be in it.
- Everything can change with the blink of an eye, but don't worry, God never blinks.
- Take a deep breath; it calms the mind.
- Get rid of anything that isn't useful. Clutter weighs you down in many ways.
- Whatever doesn't kill you really does make you stronger.
- it's never too late to be happy, but it's all up to you and no one else.
- When it comes to going after what you want in life, don't take no for an answer.
- Burn the candles, use the nice sheets. Wear fancy lingerie, don't save it for a special occasion. Today is special.
- Over-prepare then go with the flow.
- Be eccentric now; don't wait for old age to wear purple.
- The most important sex organ is the brain.
- No one is in charge of your happiness but you.
- Frame every so-called disaster with these words, "In five years, will it matter?"
- Always choose life.
- Forgive but don't forget.
- What other people think of you is none of your business.
- Time heals everything. Give time, time.

- However good or bad a situation is, it will change.
- Don't take yourself too seriously; no one else does.
- Believe in miracles.
- God loves you because of who God is, not because of anything you did or did not do.
- Don't audit life; show up and make the most of it now.
- Growing old beats the alternative – i.e. dying young.
- Your children get only one childhood.
- All that truly matters in the end is that you loved.
- Get outside every day; miracles are waiting everywhere.
- If we threw our problems in a pile and saw everyone else's, we'd grab ours back.
- Envy is a waste of time; accept what you already have, not what you think you need.
- The best has yet to come.
- No matter how you feel, get up, dress up and show up.
- Yield.
- Life isn't tied with a bow, but it's a great gift.

# BACK TO BASICS

While all this was going on I was at the same time pursuing Paddy's concept for his sludge waste recycling system and researching "anaerobic digesters" that can divert food slops into electricity. I devised the idea of collecting the food waste from local restaurants and the local hotel and putting them through an insinkerator. From there they would enter a sealed tank to produce methane. The waste material would be sent to Paddy's tank to create fuel pellets while the methane entered a turbine to produce electricity. I then had  produced my concept onto solidworks software for fabrication. My idea was fuelled by the government's drive to introduce kitchen slop buckets in every home. It involved taking food that could once only be sent to landfill and turning it into something of value on a huge scale. Suitable premises were located in South Armagh to begin the assembly of the digestor.

# PAUDRIC MOORE'S LIFE

Now on a very different note I wish to address an issue of great importance to you as a reader who may be wondering how to put your life into perspective.

In 1996 I became very ill and was hospitalized and I went through a short period of confusion but soon, through the methods described in Dr Joseph Murphy's book, *The Power of Your Sub-Conscious Mind*, I quickly healed myself of that aliment. However, since then I have been accused by the medical profession of having grandiose ideas and being all powerful, so I looked up the definition of 'grandiose' in my dictionary to discover it meant producing an imposing effect. Therefore I carried on with my goal in life and discovered through much research the harmful effects of prescription drugs which I was forced against my will to accept.

For example, in the year 2000, I found that the *Journal of the American Medical Association* published the results of a study conservatively estimating that prescription drugs accounted for more than 120,000 deaths in the United States annually and was the third leading cause of death. In 2003, another study found prescription drugs to be responsible for more deaths in the USA than anything else, including cancer and AIDS, causing more than 300,000 deaths per year.

Reflecting back now on the inception of the idea for the community peace centre in Crossmaglen, I must stress that it was an idea that anyone could have developed. In the beginning it started off simply and slowly. My first real break with it came after I read the Ray Davey story about the formation of the Corrymeela Peace Centre in Ballycastle, County Antrim, but after that came determination, definiteness of purpose, and a desire to attain my goal. Then came the persistence over 20 years. It was no ordinary desire that overcame disappointment, discouragement, temporary defeat, criticism and constant reminders that the project was a "waste of time". In fact, it was a burning desire! an obsession!

When the idea was first planted in my mind by the Ray Davey story, it was nursed, coaxed and enticed to remain alive. Gradually the idea became larger under its own power, and it coaxed, nursed and drove me. Ideas are like that: first you give them life and action and guidance, then they take on a life of their own and sweep aside all opposition.

(the Ray Davey Story)

At the start of world war two Ray was a young chaplin in Belfast N. Ireland who aspired to lend spiritual help to the troops on the front line, so he joined the YMCA and travelled to the front line where he began to administer help. He soon came under the eyes of the gastapo and was arrested and detained in Bresdin concentration camp. When in the camp he noticed how the inmates from different backgrounds and .cultures were tolerating each other and he wondered if the same could be achieved on the outside. He was in the camp the night Dresdin city was bombed and the bombing had a telling effect on him. When the war was over he returned to his native Belfast where they msde him dean of Queens University where he became terribly aware and concerned about the high level of sectarian strife in Belfast in the 60's, then in 1965 it became known to him that a site was for sale in Ballycastle Co Antrim which he purchased for £6000 and together with his students raised the money in 10 days. This was the start of what is now today the Corrymeela Peace Centre which has been visited by Mother Thersa/ the Dala Lama/ and Prince Charles.

On another occasion when I visited Paddy I found him bent over his kitchen table which had a large A1 sheet of drawing paper upon it. To it's left and right sides were a large wooden compass and protractor. He explained that he was plotting the ancient love knot of Ireland which was to be the model for the site layout of his proposed peace centre. In it's centre he placed his pyramid reception area with conference rooms and offices---along the semi-circled approach roadways he placed a series of traditional cottages---and around the Celtic circle he placed a number of respite centres ---in the grounds he had a swimming pool, museum. Workshops, tennis court,spa & sauna and tennis court. All we need now is a few million to build it Paddy said.

(to be continued as future events unfold)

# THE FOUR KINGDOMS OF IRELAND

In ancient times Ireland was divided into four kingdoms each ruled by a king with the fifth or control kingdom ruled by a high king from the palace of Tara. Although the four southern kingdoms were Celtic in character, it's still rather uncertain if the Ulster kingdom was Celtic as it seems much more likely that Ulster was made up of more ancient Irish people than the Celts. These Ulstermen, or Cruithni, were descended from the ancient pre-Celtic Irish people and considered themselves different from the rest of Ireland. So they built a border – a massive earth wall and trench that ran from Athlone through Streamstown, north east to Lough Owel, north to Lough Derravaragh and east to Telltown. However, by 300 AD this border had been pushed back. It can be traced from Bundoran in south Donegal to Loughs Melvin, Macnean and Allen and east from there to Slieve Gullion in South Armagh. Today in Armagh this border is well preserved and is known as the Pig's Dyke and the Worm's Cast.

In those days Ulster's capital was at Emania, close to Armagh city. In the 4th century there was a fight between Fergus, King of Ulster and the Ardri, who commanded his nephews, The Three Collas, to attack Ulster.

Breaking through the Dyke near Lough Muckno in Co Monaghan, they killed the Ulster King and burned the Royal Palace of Emania. They drove the Ulster people into Antrim, Down and parts of Derry. These daring Ulstermen then divided themselves into the two kingdoms of Dalriada and Dalaradia. The Dalradains, masters of Down and South Antrim, built new fortifications. Known as the Dane's Cast, it runs from the western side of the Newry River near Meigh to Goraghwood and Poyntzpass, ending in Scarva.

(Reprinted by kind permission of Ireland's Own magazine.)

# Paddy's Parting Words (as Dictated by Himself)

There are many English and many Anglo-Irish people who think, merely from ignorance, that Ireland was a barbarous and half-savage country before the English came among the people and civilised them. This little book has been written and published with the main object of spreading as widely as possible among our people, young and old, a knowledge of the civilisation and general social condition of Crossmaglen, South Armagh, Ireland. This publication comes at an appropriate time, when there is an awakening of interest in the language dialect, and in Irish lore of every kind, unparalleled in our history. This book, so far as it finds its way among the two classes above mentioned, will, I fancy, open their eyes somewhat. It is the intention of this publication to shed some light on the importance of preserving our heritage and culture. In the opening preface you will have read the remarks of a well-informed Englishman writing in 1890 about us Irish, and as far back as 300 years ago the English poet Edmund Spencer, who lived for some time in Ireland, made himself well acquainted with its history. He knew what it was in the past ages; so that in one of his poems he speaks of the time

"When Ireland flourished in fame
Of wealth and goodnesse, far above the rest
Of all that beare the British Islands name "

This book is intending to trigger a positive spark in the lives and mind of all persons interested in equality and justice for all. I have done my best to make it readable and interesting, as well as instructive. The ordinary history of our country has been written by many, and the reader has a wide choice. But this book of mine has, for the first and only time, brought within reach of the general public a knowledge of the whole social life of Crossmaglen, and it gives in simple, plain language an account of the condition of our community in days now gone up to the present.

So now I, Paddy, want to give of myself and I want to share if there is an opportunity to change or inspire others. The more I share my stories the more I inspect my past and learn to let go. To be happy or to continue in a life of drudgery is only a choice for us all to decide. Our lives let us make our own decision; we must choose to accept all the different parts of ourselves, our small characteristics, the screwups, the things we may not do too well, and to praise ourselves when the time is right. I hope this story of mine will inspire you to do what it is you need to do to get you to where it is you want to go. Changing your life IS possible! I am convinced you CAN do it and make things come true for you just like I did. You will be anxious to get to the next stage right now if you are willing and ready to take action to change.

Now in passing let me add that I have been emboldened to reduce my experience to the printed page, because I am now less concerned about what "they say" than I was in the years past. One of the blessings of maturity is that it sometimes brings one greater courage to be truthful, regardless of what those who do not understand, may think or say.

## Go, little book

Go, little book,
Among this universe
Of foes and friends
And when in Lissaraw Street
Again we meet
One question I will ask of you
And record with pen
Your readers round this world:
Did they laugh "WITH" Crossmaglen?

# Thank You

And now in closing I want to personally thank you for having contributed to our cause. By doing so you have left a legacy for your children and grandchildren to visit Crossmaglen, where, by purchasing and reading my book, you have made it possible to create a Global House of Peace. A Community Peace Centre that was the dream of yesterday and the hope of today, shall now become the reality of tomorrow. God Bless you, dear reader, and make sure in this life that you

*Be all that you can because that's all of you there is.*

May the Peace of Christ be with you, and may the road always rise up to meet you and may the wind be always at your back, and may you be in Heaven half an hour before the devil knows you're dead.

### Patrick McEntegart

You can contact me at 37 Lissaraw Road, Crossmaglen, Newry, Co Down N Ireland BT35 9HT or by email crossmaglen1946@gmail.com

# About the Author: Patrick McEntegart

I am a 71-year-old single parent with 9 beautiful grandchildren, born and bred in Crossmaglen where I lived for 40 years before emigrating to America. I lived there for 15 years and have been back in Crossmaglen these past 12 years or more. My work has been in many fields, from educating, construction, professional consulting, project management, motivational speaking and designing. I presently own a construction company which has built high-rise apartment blocks in Manhattan.

So why do I write? I feel the need to express myself and to help improve my native community. Being very creative by nature, I have done many things which exemplify my need to be original. I am a true Aquarius, often walking to the beat of my own drum, a rebel, in many ways, stretching ahead of the norm in my thinking at times. Reflecting back to my school days, I remember my master telling me I'd be picking praties all my life. He also said I couldn't write. He differed greatly from my role model and neighbour, John Feeney, who said I would accomplish great things. Feeney's is where I worked long years ago. I locked horns with the schoolmaster who said I couldn't write, in his opinion. It has not stopped me from writing and having some of my work published. The quality might not be what my master was used to, or perhaps it might have improved greatly since he made that remark. Regardless, I write for myself and in doing so I hope others will enjoy it, finding meaning and humour in my words and work.

# APPENDIX

Page 44;            International handbook of surveying by
                    Ed de Leeuw

Page 44;            land surveying ref manual by Andrew L Harbin

Page 43;            how precision engineers created the modern world
                    by Simon Winchester

Page 51;            text the secret languages of Ireland by
                    R A Stewart McAlister

Pages 252—262;  some things of importance to Ireland NYPL.

Pages 255—260;  awful conditions and prospects In county Mayo by
                    Eneas Mac Donnell, esq 1849.

www.ingramcontent.com/pod-product-compliance
Lightning Source LLC
Chambersburg PA
CBHW051155120626
46547CB00012B/1076